Foundational Drumming
Level 1
Lessons for the Drum Set

Michael Charleston

SIDE NOTE
Music Publications

5267 Warner Ave Suite #336
Huntington Beach, CA 92649
sidenotemusic.com
© 2010, 2015 Michael Charleston

Foundational Drumming, Level 1, Third Edition

Published By:

SideNote Music Publications
5267 Warner Ave Suite #336
Huntington Beach, CA 92649 U.S.A.
(714) 492-7547
sidenotemusic.com
foundationaldrumming.com

All rights reserved. No part of this textbook may be reproduced, recreated or transmitted in any form or by any means, electronic or mechanical, including photocopying, without written permission from the author.

ISBN 10: 0-9861758-0-3
ISBN 13: 978-0-9861758-0-0

© 2010, 2015 by Michael Charleston.
Printed in the United States of America.

The *Percussive Arts Society 40 International Drum Rudiments* featured in this book have been reprinted by the permission of the Percussive Arts Society, Inc., 32 E. Washington, Suite 1400, Indianapolis, IN 46204-3516;
E-mail: **percarts@pas.org**; Web: **www.pas.org**

Acknowledgments

Foundational Drumming represents a collaborative effort from several groups of individuals, without whom this series likely wouldn't exist. I would like to mostly thank the hundreds of students that I had the honor of working with from 2004 onwards. Many of these students unknowingly served as test subjects for this material, and the concept of having a multi-level drum set series was born out of the continuous observation of their progress. I would also like to thank the many instructors I had growing up who not only taught me to play the drums, but instilled the desire to teach others. These teachers include Richard Charleston (my father and first drum teacher), Carmine Appice, John Schutza, Lee Nichols, Jason Lingle and Keith Harris.

About the Author

Michael Charleston is a professional drummer and music educator from Orange County, California. He has worked with hundreds of students in the Southern California area. Since 2005, Michael's textbooks, worksheets, tests, solos, and charts have been used by dozens of local music academies, conservatories, music programs, summer camps, and private drum instructors to great success. Michael teaches both private lessons and group classes at several facilities in Orange County, and lessons can be booked with him at *takelessons.com*.

Table Of Contents

Introduction — 5

Section 1: Single Line Rhythms — 7

Table of Time 9
The Percussive Arts Society International Drum Rudiments 10
Lesson 1: Quarter Notes and Eighth Notes 12
Lesson 2: Rests 15
Lesson 3: Sixteenth Notes 19
Lesson 4: Rudiments and Sticking Patterns 23

Section 2: Drum Set Grooves — 27

Quickly Building a Backbeat Groove 28
Notation Examples 30
Lesson 5: Eighth Notes on the Hi-Hat 31
Lesson 6: Quarter Notes on the Hi-Hat 36
Lesson 7: Off-Beat Eighth Notes on the Hi-Hat 39
Lesson 8: Sixteenth Notes on the Hi-Hat 41
Journey Through The Rhythms Exercise 43
Lesson 9: Rhythmic Feel Variations 48

Section 3: Accessories — 53

Lesson 10: Playing the Crash Cymbal 54
Lesson 11: Opening the Hi-Hat 57
Lesson 12: Fills 61

Table Of Contents | *Foundational Drumming, Level 1*

Section 4: Drum Set Solos — 69

- A Simple Dish 70
- Joy Ride 70
- A License To Drive 71
- The Sloth 71
- 25 Cents 72
- A Quick Switch 72
- Sector 7 73
- Somewhere In Time 74
- The Dryer 75
- Hearing Voices 76
- The Graduation 77
- Space Maintainer 78

Completion Checklist — 79

Introduction

Designed as an expandable curriculum for use in private lessons and group classes, *Foundational Drumming, Level 1* presents basic drum set material to the *very beginning student* - defined here as a student with little or no experience playing the drums or reading drum set notation. The material works best under the guidance of a teacher, who can not only demonstrate the concepts featured in this book, but also customize and expand upon exercises and applications, depending on the age and ability of the student.

Foundational Drumming, Level 1 is divided into twelve lessons. Although the lessons are labeled numerically and become progressively more challenging from lesson to lesson, the material does not need to be played in order, and concepts from multiple lessons can often be learned simultaneously.

With the completion of this book, the very beginning student can expect to:

- Play and identify several rudiments, including the single stroke roll, the paradiddle, and the flam.

- Understand the very basics of rhythm and snare drum notation, with a focus on quarter, eighth, and sixteenth note groupings.

- Read and play a wide range of drum set grooves using four distinct hi-hat rhythms.

- Access and expand upon a large vocabulary of basic drum set fills.

- Articulate and enhance grooves by playing the crash cymbal, opening the hi-hat, or altering the consistent placement of the snare drum.

- Begin playing in a multitude of musical environments.

- Begin reading basic drum set compositions.

- Build a *basic foundation* that will aid and promote the student's ability to continuously study the drum set effectively.

Introduction | *Foundational Drumming, Level 1*

■ The Metronome

The tempo of the metronome, as well as its inclusion within exercises and solos, should fall under the discretion of the teacher. While the metronome is usually assigned to count quarter notes and effectively serve as a *pulse*, it might make sense to occasionally double the tempo, or set the metronome to count eighth notes instead. As playing with a metronome for the first time can often be difficult for the new student, providing more "timing reference points" is very effective.

■ Drum Set Staff and Configuration

The material of this book is designed to be played on the most basic drum set possible, seen below as a *four-piece* with a ride cymbal, a hi-hat, and one crash cymbal. Depending on the access to additional gear, other drum set components, such as an additional rack tom or crash cymbal, can be added to exercises.

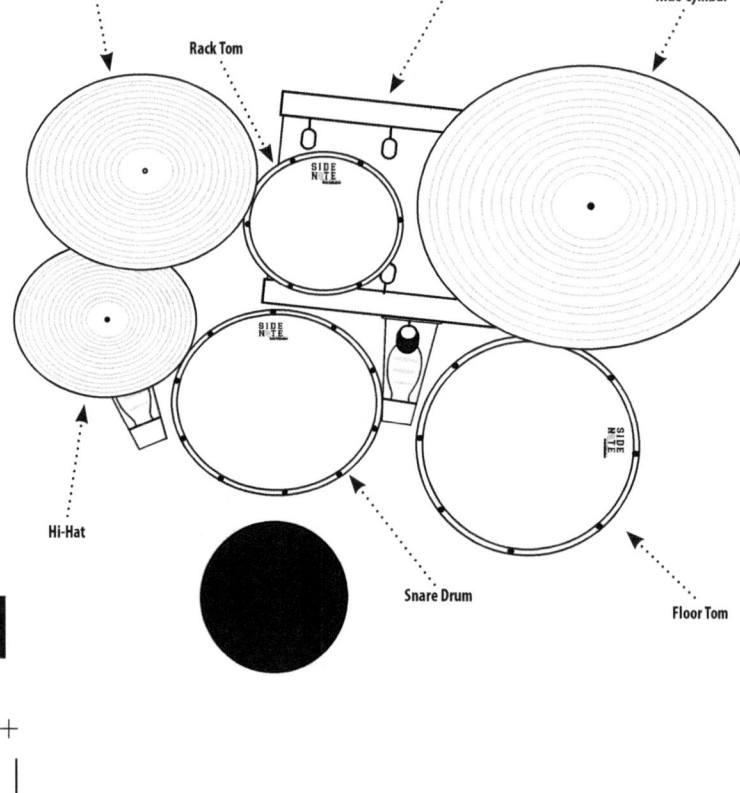

The drum set staff seen below represents what I believe to be the most common drum set notation used today; however, it should be noted that unlike melodic music, drum music is *not* universal. The placement of drum components on the staff will ultimately come down to the choice made by the individual composer.

Most of this book features *single voice notation* with the stems facing up. Examples of alternate notation are provided on page 30.

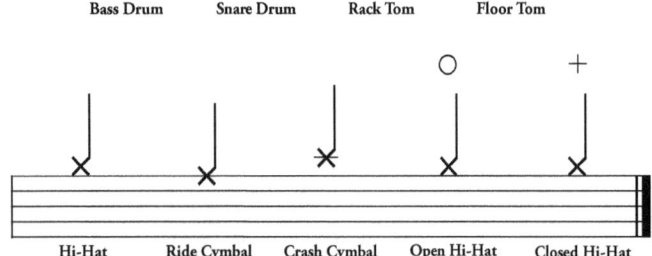

SECTION 1

Single Line Rhythms

Lessons 1 - 4

Rhythm, in its simplest form, represents repeated events on a scale of time. These events can be labeled as sounds (notes) and silence (rests) that combine to create a unique pattern or phrase. Chances are that you unknowingly display rhythm on an almost daily basis; clapping your hands or tapping your feet along to music, counting along with the seconds of a clock, and even uttering a sports team cheer like "*2, 4, 6, 8, who do we appreciate*" - these activities all showcase the consistently marked points in time that define rhythm.

As drum set music divides different rhythms and drum set components over multiple lines of a staff, this section will be focusing on rhythms presented on a *single line*. Due to this, the exercises of this section only require the hands to practice, and can be played solely on a practice pad (recommended), or a snare drum. A lot of this section can even be practiced simply by clapping and counting out loud.

■ Establishing a Pulse and Discovering Quarter Notes

In most music, a **pulse** can be indentified almost immediately as a *constant and consistent marking of time within a song*. The natural way most people tap their feet along to music almost always indentifies the pulse. The speed of this pulse will be referred to as **tempo**, and each count or foot tap is called a **beat**. Numbers have been assigned to these beats, and as seen below, *four beats are counted before resetting and counting to four again*. A good starting point is to simply count to four, evenly and consistently.

1 → 2 → 3 → 4 → 1 → 2 → 3 → 4 →

As the pulse has been indentified as a looped set of four beats, a symbol will be placed on these beats that allow for the written notation of this pulse. These symbols are referred to as **quarter notes**, which represent one fourth of a full and complete count. When you tap your foot along to music, there is a good chance that you are tapping quarter notes.

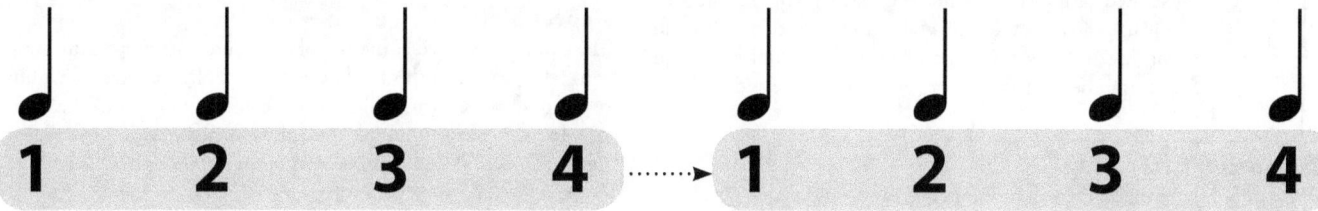

7

Section 1 | Single Line Rhythms | *Lessons 1 - 4*

Featured below is a five-line staff, used almost universally in music notation. While in melodic music each line represents a different pitch, in drum set music each line represents a different component of the drum set. As the material of this section will only be focusing on single line rhythms, the quarter notes will be assigned to the space designated for the *snare drum*.

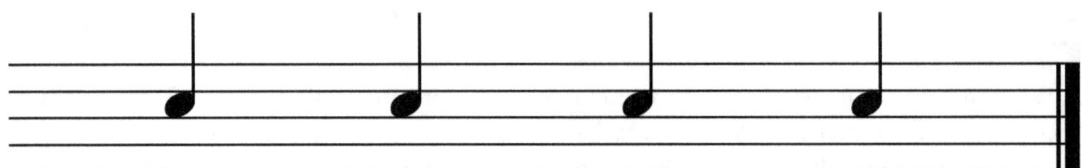

Batches of beats are contained within a **measure** or **bar**. Measures are separated by bar lines, which signify the end of one measure and the beginning of a new measure.

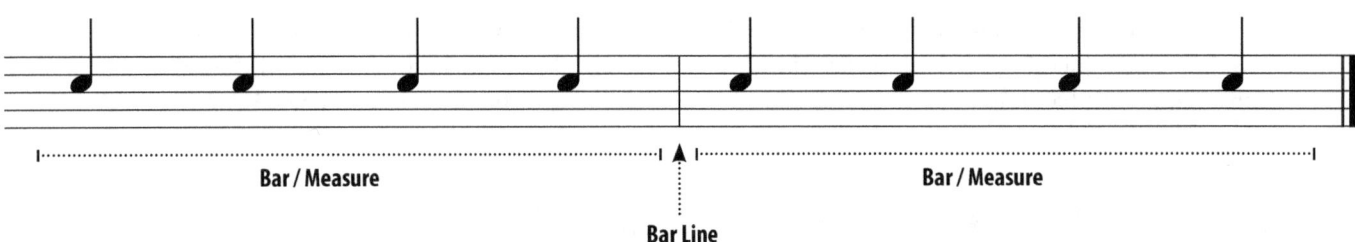

Bar / Measure   Bar / Measure

Bar Line

Measures also come with a set of instructions that can determine what type of instrument notation will be used, the way in which the measures should be counted, and whether or not to repeat.

Time Signature
The time signature determines how many beats will be included in each measure. The bottom number represents the type of note, seen here as a quarter note represented by the number '4'. The top number tells us *how many* of those notes will be in each measure before a new measure is started. In a 4/4 time signature, there are *four quarter notes per measure*.

Double Bar Line
The double bar line usually states that a passage or composition has ended. Repeat signs are often contained within these double bar lines.

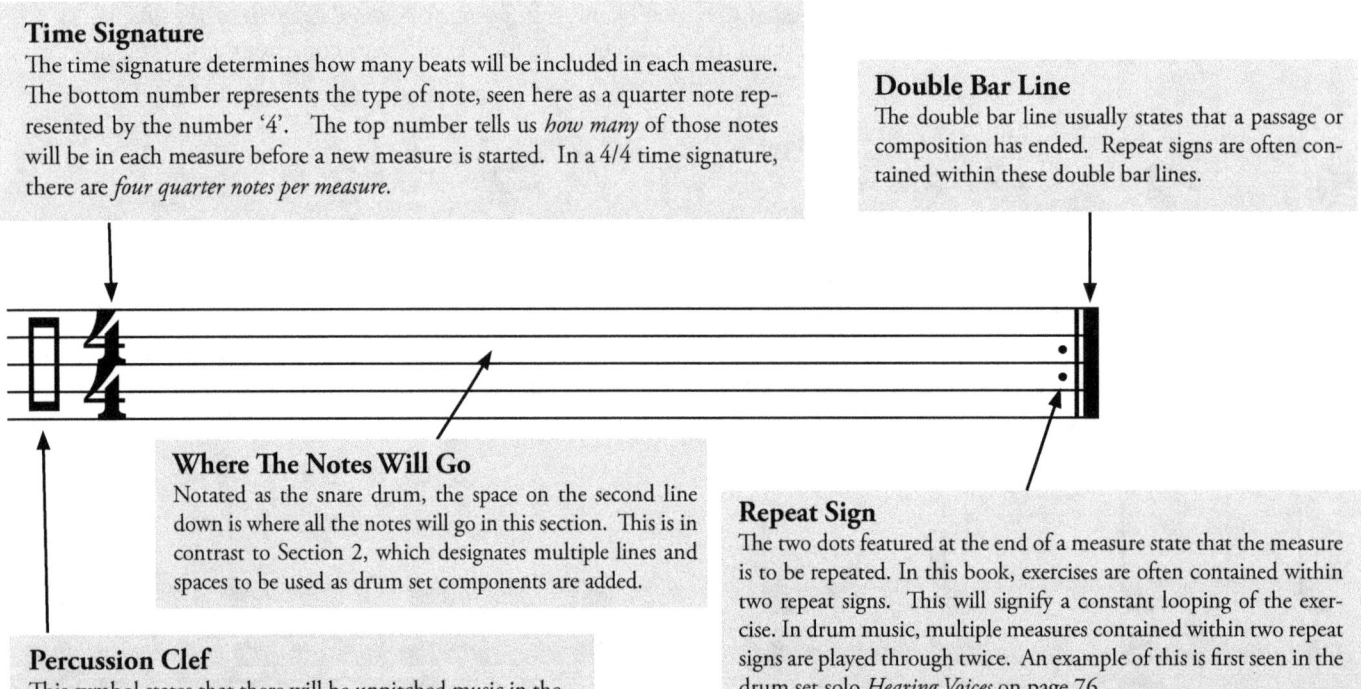

Where The Notes Will Go
Notated as the snare drum, the space on the second line down is where all the notes will go in this section. This is in contrast to Section 2, which designates multiple lines and spaces to be used as drum set components are added.

Repeat Sign
The two dots featured at the end of a measure state that the measure is to be repeated. In this book, exercises are often contained within two repeat signs. This will signify a constant looping of the exercise. In drum music, multiple measures contained within two repeat signs are played through twice. An example of this is first seen in the drum set solo *Hearing Voices* on page 76.

Percussion Clef
This symbol states that there will be unpitched music in the measures. Often called a *neutral clef* and most commonly seen in drum notation.

Section 1 | Single Line Rhythms | *Lessons 1 - 4*

■ Table of Time

The table of time below shows the relation between all types of note divisions used in this book and highlights the big three: *quarter notes, eighth notes* and *sixteenth notes*.

■ Rudiments Used

The *P.A.S 40 International Snare Drum Rudiments* are included on the next two pages and highlight the specific rudiments that will be presented in Lesson 4. While not every rudiment concept will make it to the drum set in this level, several of the rudiments learned here, mainly the *double stroke roll* and the *three paradiddles*, provide excellent practice material for the new student. Under the guidance of a teacher, these rudiments can be continuously practiced and refined on a practice pad or snare drum.

Percussive Arts Society International Drum Rudiments

All rudiments should be practiced: open (slow) to close (fast) to open (slow) and/or at an even moderate march tempo.

I. ROLL RUDIMENTS

A. Single Stroke Roll Rudiments

1. Single Stroke Roll *
2. Single Stroke Four
3. Single Stroke Seven

B. Multiple Bounce Roll Rudiments

4. Multiple Bounce Roll
5. Triple Stroke Roll

C. Double Stroke Open Roll Rudiments

6. Double Stroke Open Roll *
7. Five Stroke Roll *
8. Six Stroke Roll
9. Seven Stroke Roll *
10. Nine Stroke Roll *
11. Ten Stroke Roll *
12. Eleven Stroke Roll *
13. Thirteen Stroke Roll *
14. Fifteen Stroke Roll *
15. Seventeen Stroke Roll

II. DIDDLE RUDIMENTS

16. Single Paradiddle *
17. Double Paradiddle *
18. Triple Paradiddle
19. Single Paradiddle-diddle

* These rudiments are also included in the original Standard 26 American Drum Rudiments.

Copyright © 1984 by the Percussive Arts Society™, 110 W. Washington Street, Suite A, Indianapolis, IN 46204
International Copyright Secured   All Rights Reserved

III. FLAM RUDIMENTS

20. Flam *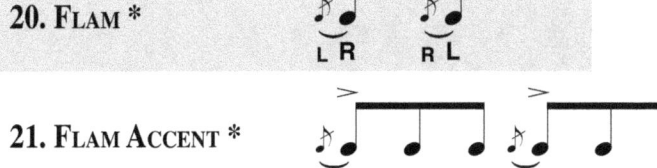

21. Flam Accent *

22. Flam Tap *

23. Flamacue *

24. Flam Paradiddle *

25. Single Flammed Mill

26. Flam Paradiddle-diddle *

27. Pataflafla

28. Swiss Army Triplet

29. Inverted Flam Tap

30. Flam Drag

IV. DRAG RUDIMENTS

31. Drag *

32. Single Drag Tap *

33. Double Drag Tap *

34. Lesson 25 *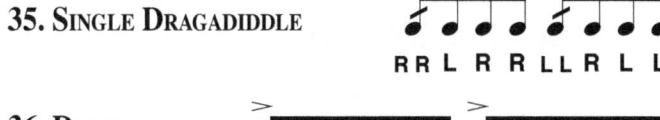

35. Single Dragadiddle

36. Drag Paradiddle #1 *

37. Drag Paradiddle #2 *

38. Single Ratamacue *

39. Double Ratamacue *

40. Triple Ratamacue *

Lesson 1
Quarter Notes and Eighth Notes

Designating a note to be played on the *off-beat*, eighth notes allow for the spaces between the quarter note beats to be accounted for. While initially given as a common set of two, four consecutive eighth notes can optionally be joined to share a beam, seen in the example below. Both styles of eighth notes are featured in this book, and are equally common in notated drum music.

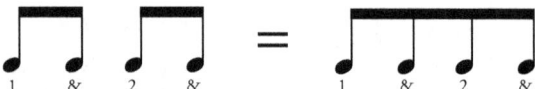

Counting Eighth Notes

Counting eighth notes entails adding an "and" between each quarter note beat, represented in this book as the symbol '**&**'. Remember - every beat has the same length and value, and the verbal counting of each beat should be even and consistent.

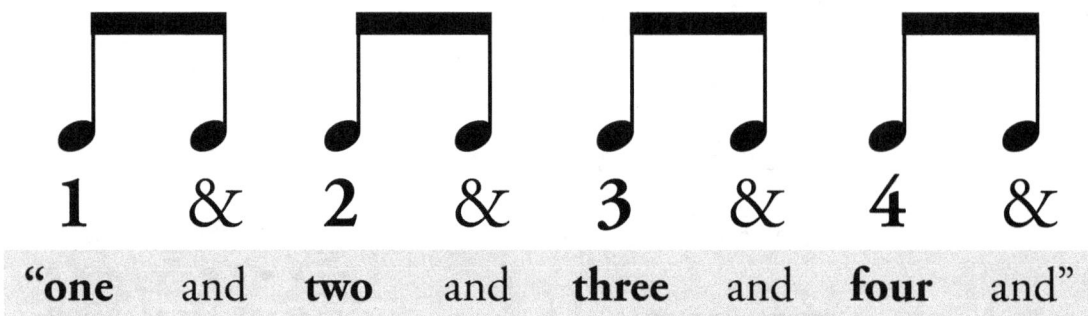

Sticking Patterns

A sticking pattern determines which hand will play on which note. While sticking patterns are secondary to the purpose of this section (which is a fundamental understanding of basic rhythm), they are provided for exercises in Lessons 1 - 3, and are further discussed in Lesson 4. The following three lessons will utilize a *standard sticking pattern*, in which the right hand plays *on* the beat (quarter notes) while the left hand plays *off* the beat (eighth notes). Examples A - E on the following page demonstrate this concept.

Lesson 1 | Quarter Notes and Eighth Notes

◼ Combining Quarters and Eighths

Several examples have been provided to demonstrate the rhythmic differences between quarter notes and eighth notes. Example A should be practiced by tapping quarter notes while *counting* eighth notes. This will constitute playing *only when the numbers are spoken*. Example B features a tap on every spoken eighth note, ideally counting at the same tempo as in example A.

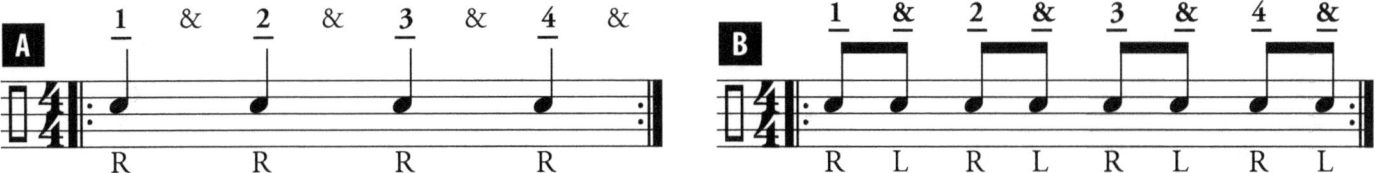

Combining both A and B, example C features one measure of quarter notes followed by one measure of eighth notes. The verbal counting of the eighth notes should be kept the same between both measures.

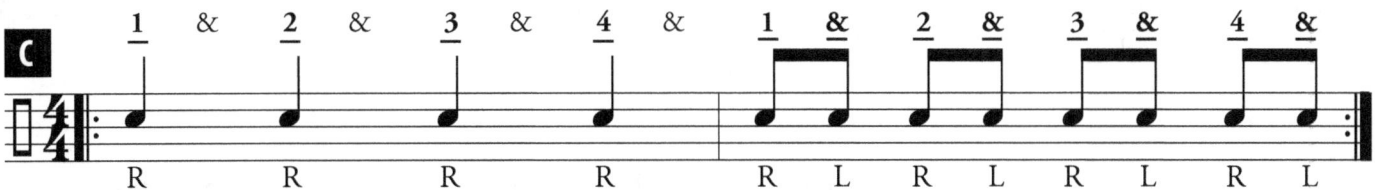

◼ Building a Unique Measure

As both quarter notes and eighth notes become comfortable to count and distinguish from each other, unique rhythms can be constructed by randomizing their placement in a 4/4 measure. Think of four *slots* - each slot can contain one quarter note or two eighth notes.

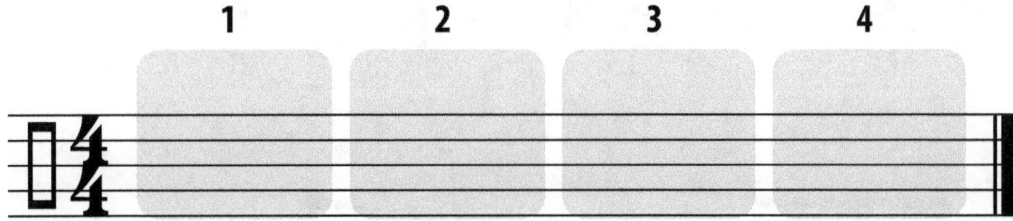

The two examples below demonstrate the simplicity of "filling the slots." As before, only the underlined beats are played while eighth notes are counted out loud.

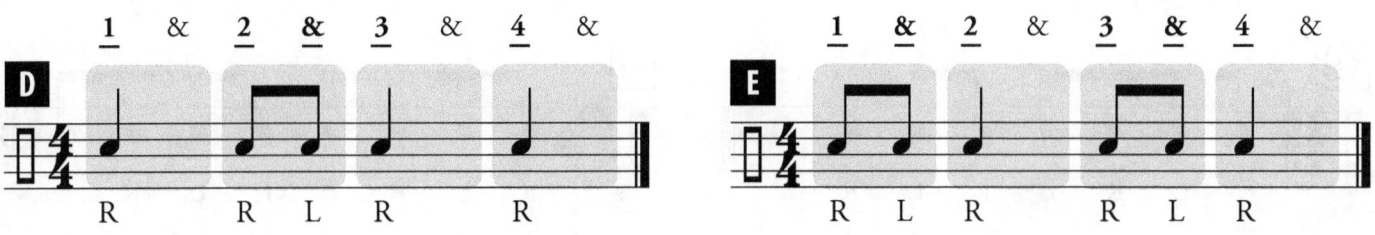

Lesson 1 | Quarter Notes and Eighth Notes

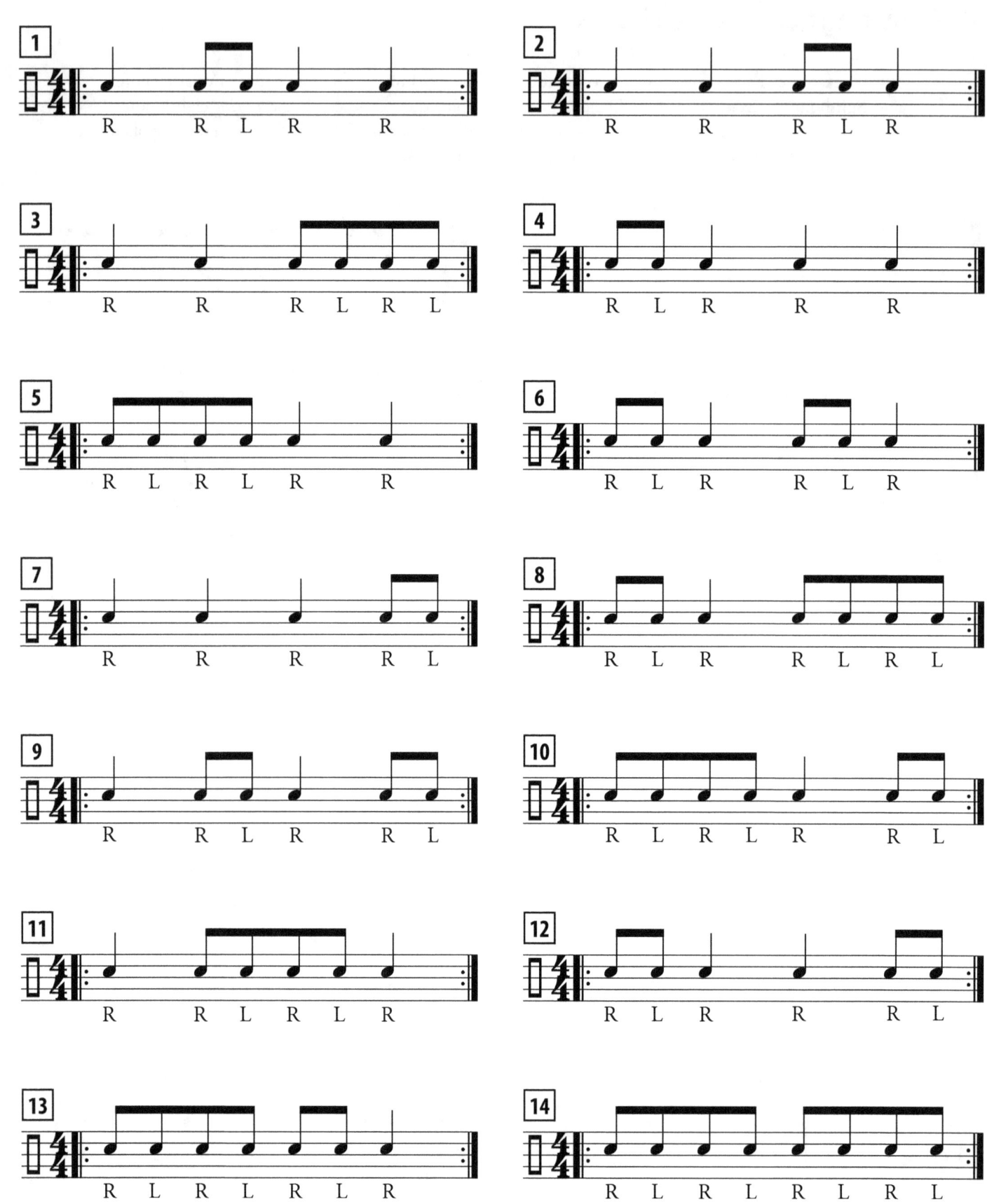

Lesson 2
Rests

A rest in rhythm represents the act of not playing for a designated amount of time. For every note that exists, there is a silent counterpart worth the same value.

Quarter Note Rests

A quarter note rest is the silent equivalent of a single quarter note, and represents the act of not playing for the length of one beat.

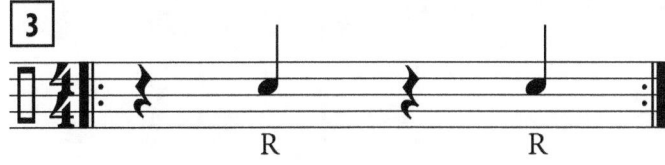

Lesson 2 | Rests

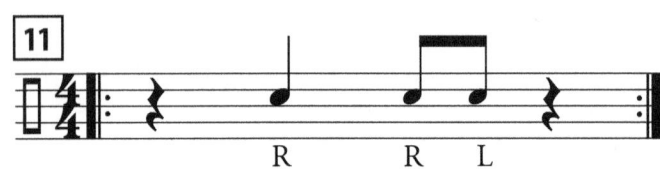
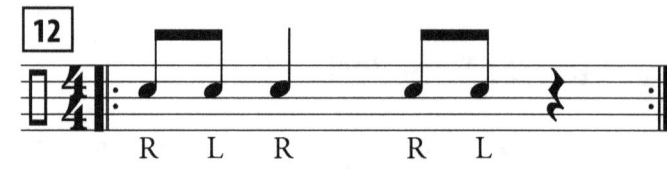

▪ Eighth Note Rests

An eighth note rest is the silent equivalent of a single eighth note. In this book, the eighth note rest will be placed exclusively on the beat, with a single eighth note placed on the adjacent '&'. When played consistently in this way, they are often referred to as *off-beat eighth notes*.

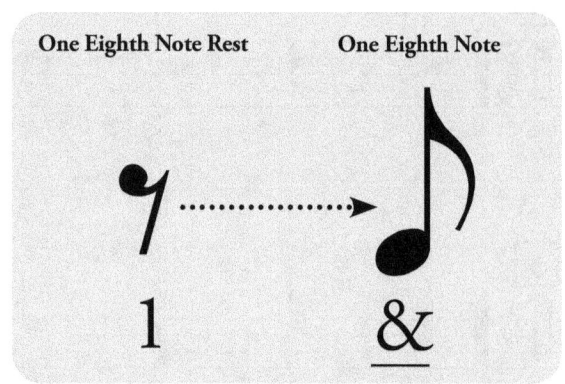

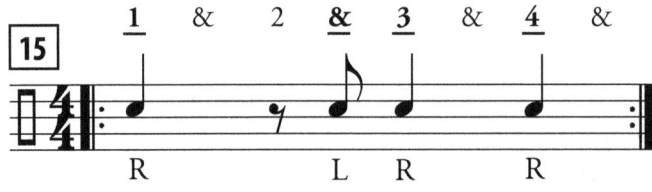
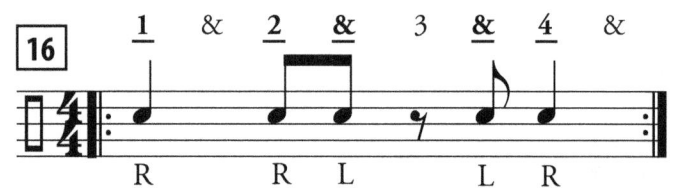

Lesson 2 | Rests

Lesson 2 | Rests

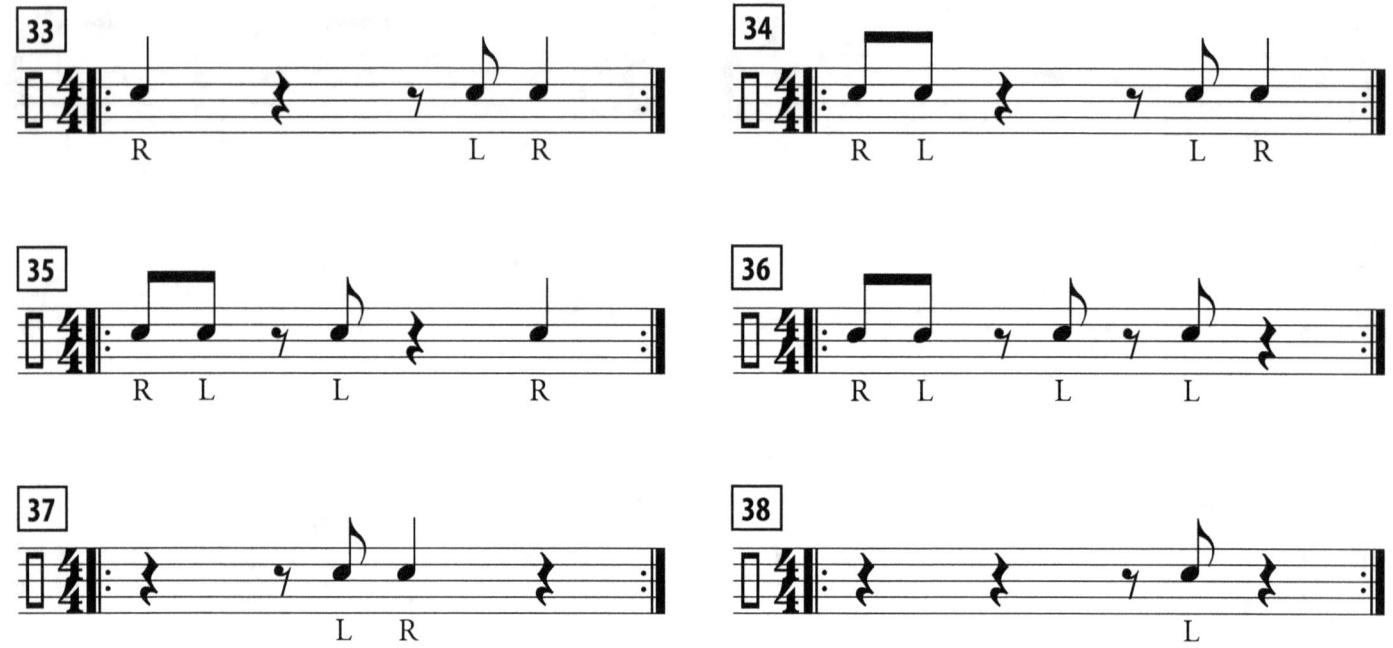

Whole Note and Half Note Rests

Exercise #39 features an example of both whole note and half note rests. Rests of this length can be thought of as *how long to wait before playing*.

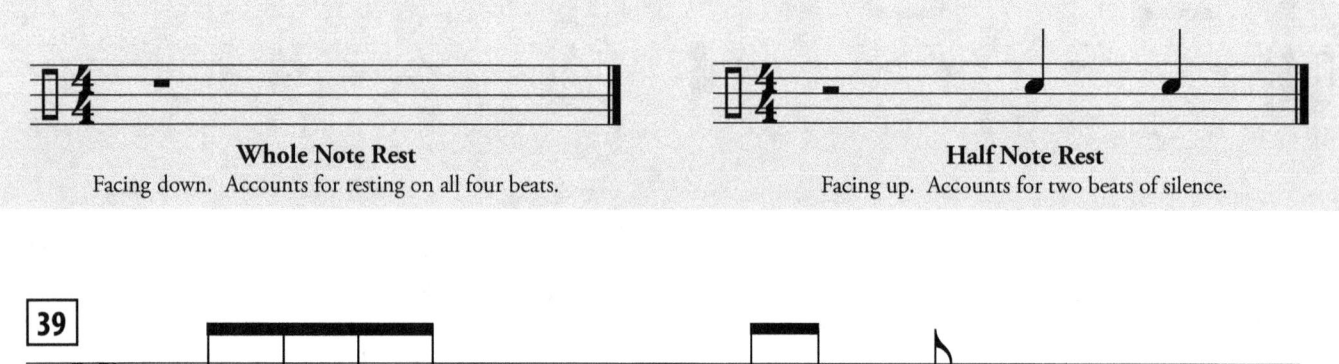

Whole Note Rest
Facing down. Accounts for resting on all four beats.

Half Note Rest
Facing up. Accounts for two beats of silence.

Lesson 3
Sixteenth Notes

Sixteenth notes allow for the spaces between the eighth note beats to be accounted for, and are seen here as a common set of four. All sixteenth notes will be kept in these four-note batches at this level.

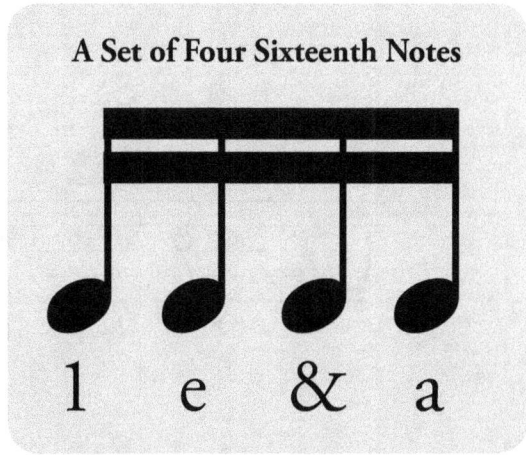

Counting Sixteenth Notes

Counting sixteenth notes entails adding an **e** (spoken as "ee") and an **a** (spoken as "uh") to the spaces between the eighth note beats. This results in *four sixteenth notes for every one quarter note*.

Building Measures using Sixteenth Notes

As sixteenth notes, eighth notes, and quarter notes become comfortable to count and distinguish from each other, unique rhythms can be constructed by randomizing their placement in a 4/4 measure. Several examples have been provided on the following page to demonstrate the rhythmic differences between each note value.

Lesson 3 | Sixteenth Notes

While example A features a beat played on every spoken sixteenth note, examples B and C should be practiced by playing *only* the underlined beats, while continuing to count sixteenth notes out loud.

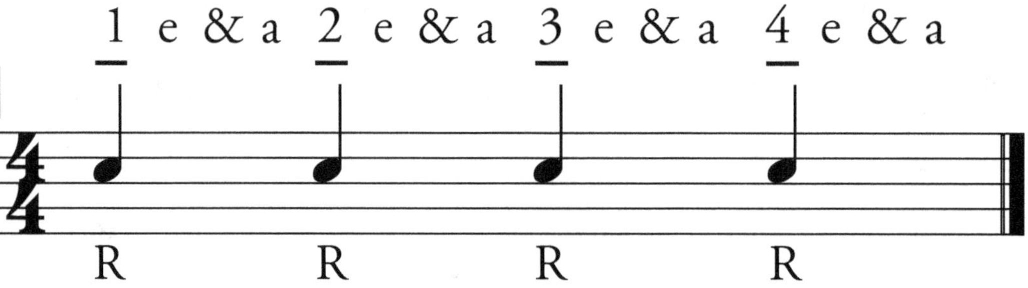

Examples D and E randomize the placement of either one quarter note, two eighth notes, or four sixteenth notes.

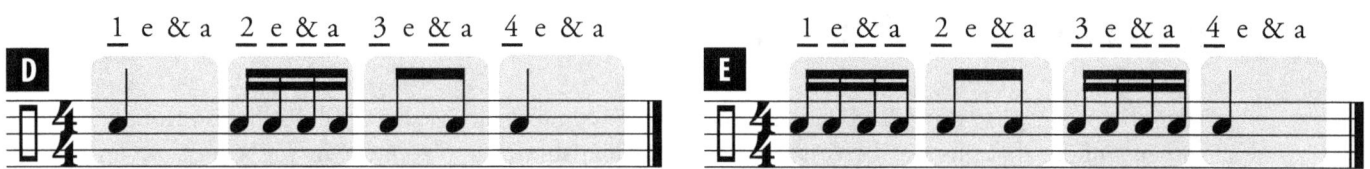

For the following twenty-eight exercises, it is advised that *full sixteenth notes continue be counted* for the duration of the measure, until each note value can be instinctively felt.

Lesson 3 | Sixteenth Notes

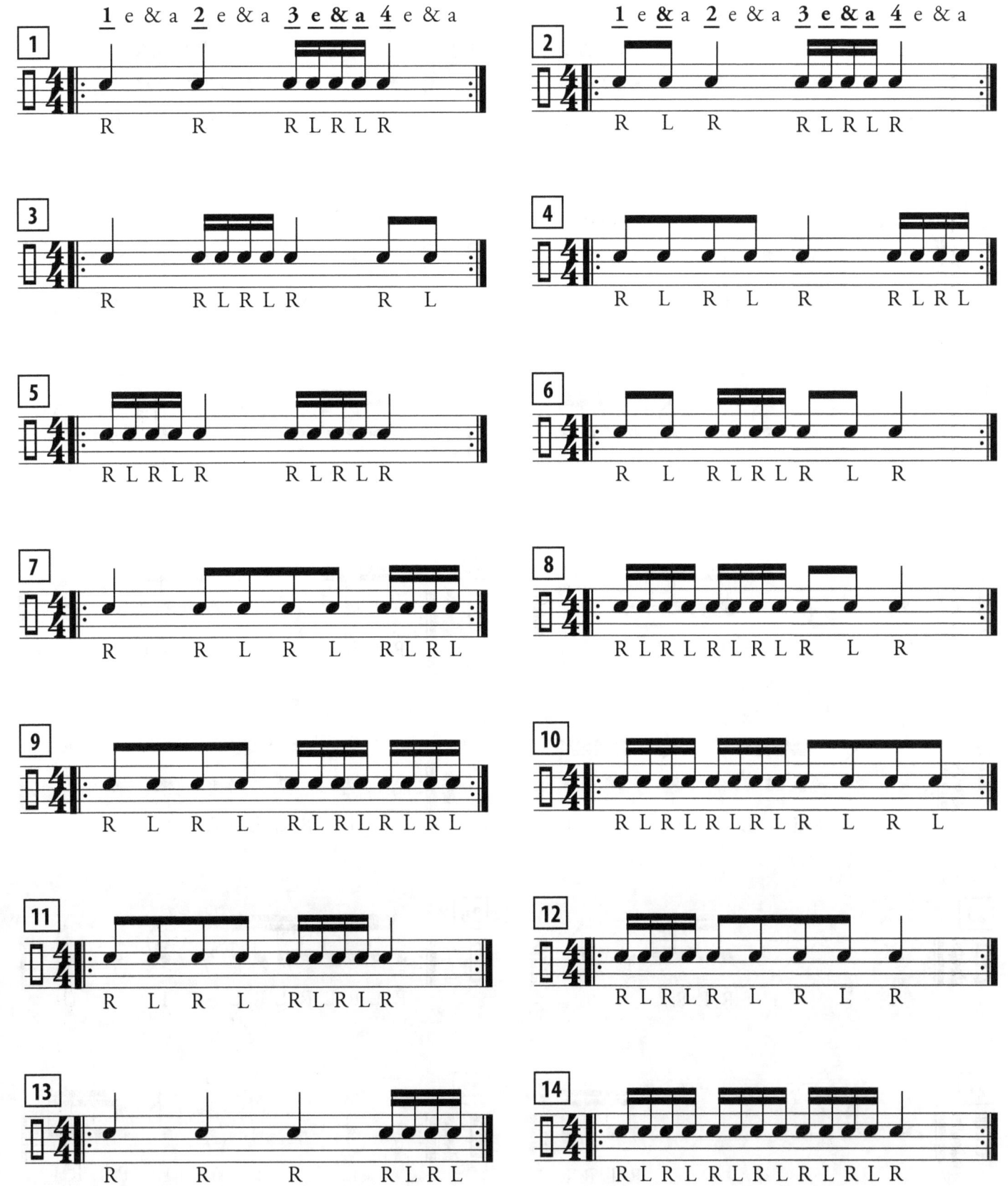

Lesson 3 | Sixteenth Notes

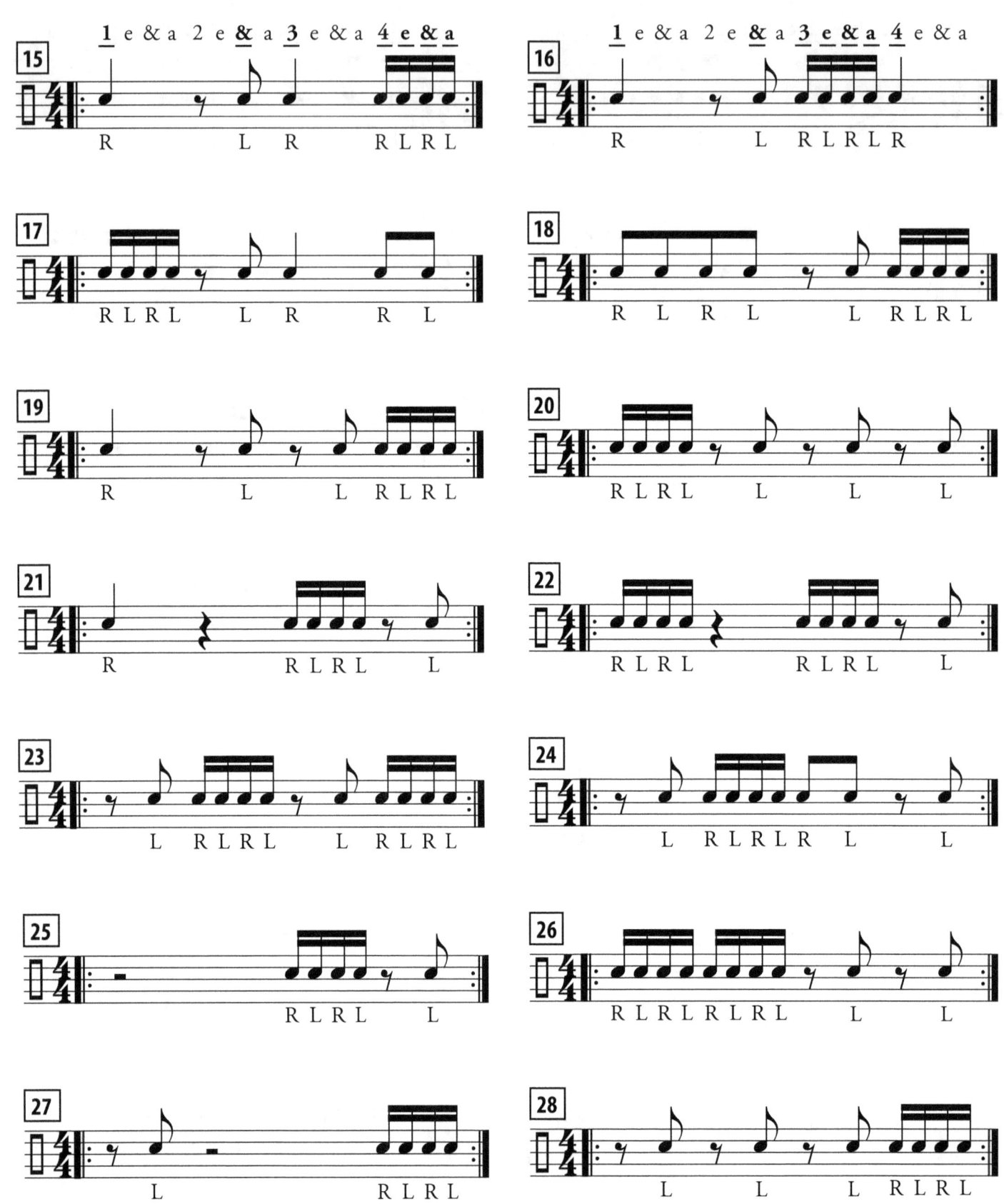

Lesson 4
Rudiments and Sticking Patterns

This lesson features six rudiments from the *P.A.S. 40 International Snare Drum Rudiments*, found on pages 10 and 11, and will focus on their associated sticking patterns. A *sticking pattern* determines which hand will play on a given note.

■ The Single Stroke Roll

The single stroke roll features a constant **R L R L** pattern played with the hands. While it is natively printed as a set of thirty-second notes on page 10, the single strokes below have been given as suggestively slower quarter, eighth, or sixteenth notes.

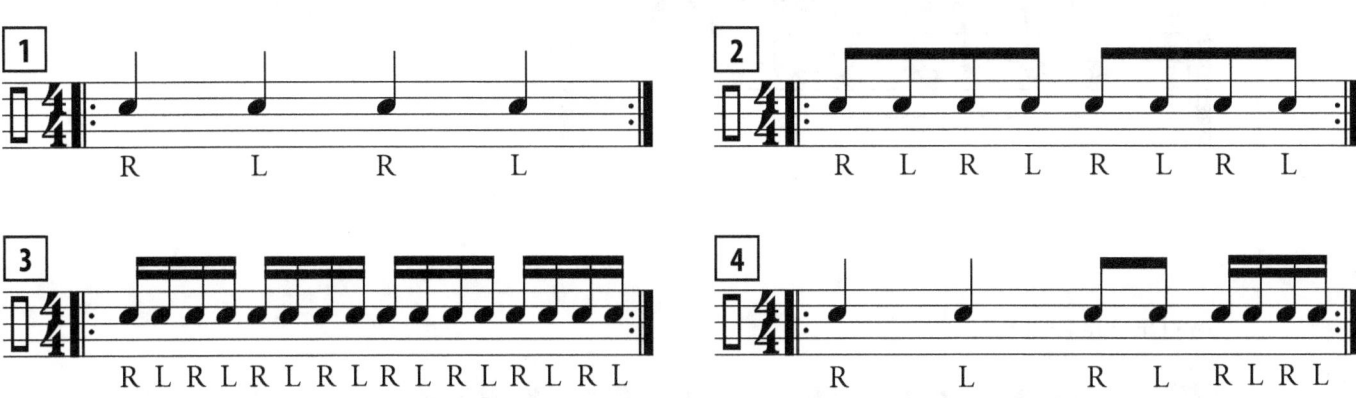

■ The Double Stroke Roll

The double stroke roll features a constant **R R L L** pattern played with the hands. While this rudiment is printed as a *roll* on page 10, the exercises below have been displayed as eighth or sixteenth notes, and are intended to initially be played slowly.

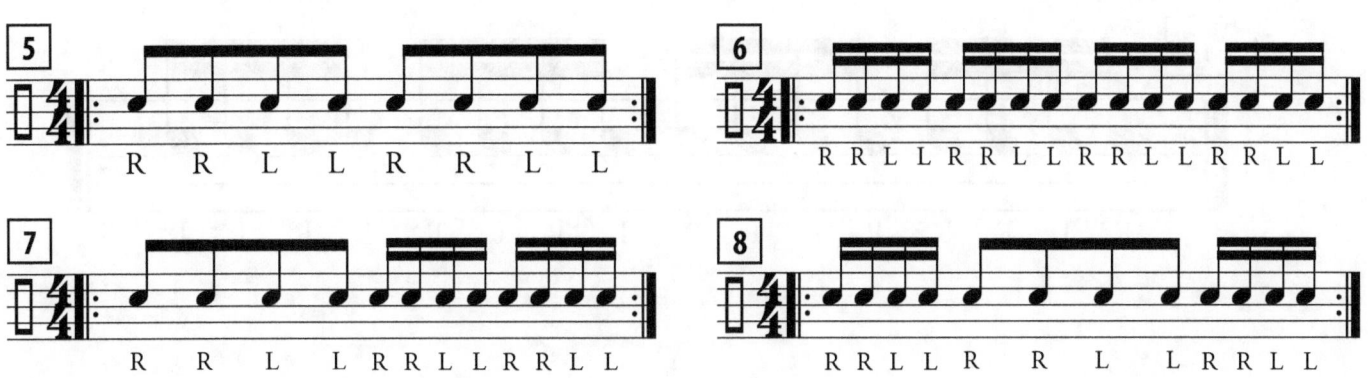

Lesson 4 | Rudiments and Sticking Patterns

Diddle Rudiments

A diddle signifies that two notes of the same hand are played in a row. The *diddle rudiments* section of the rudiment list on page 10 presents combinations of alternating strokes (**R L**) and diddles (**R R**) to create *paradiddles*. The double and triple variations each add another set of alternating strokes. As with many of the rudiments, the term paradiddle features syllables that completely suggest the sound of the rudiment, spoken as *par-a-did-dle*.

The Single Paradiddle

R L R R L R L L

The Double Paradiddle

R L R L R R   L R L R L L

The Triple Paradiddle

R L R L R L R R   L R L R L R L L

Lesson 4 | Rudiments and Sticking Patterns

The *Three Paradiddles Exercise*

The exercise below features a continuous transitioning between the three paradiddle rudiments. As all notes are played at the same tempo and with the same rhythmic value, the ability to play the proper sticking pattern for each corresponding paradiddle should be carefully observed.

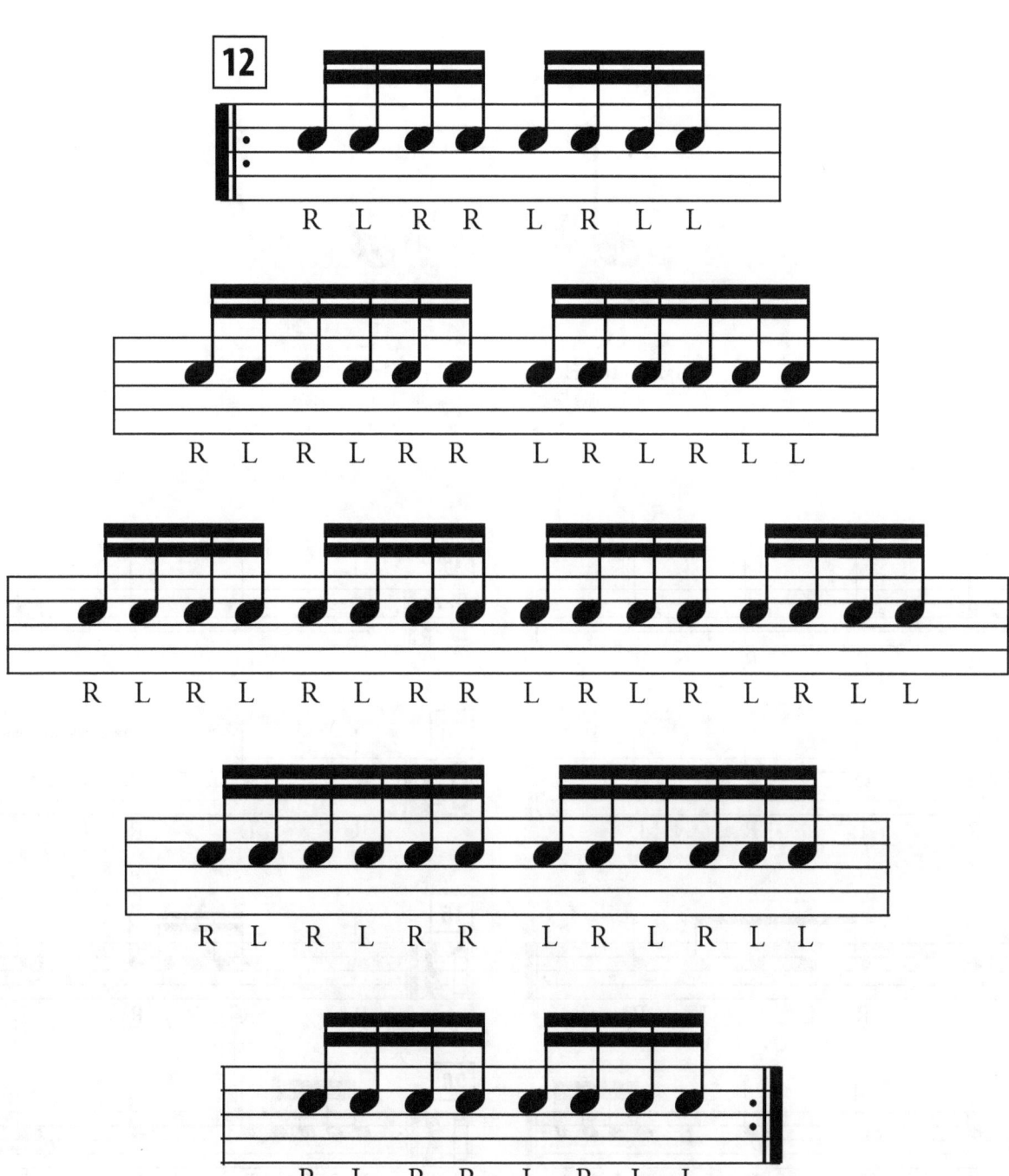

Lesson 4 | Rudiments and Sticking Patterns

■ The Flam

A flam consists of two strokes played almost simultaneously with both hands, in an effort to produce one single *thick strike*. At this level, the flam is introduced mainly as an enhancement to the drum set fills found in Lesson 12, and while both the right and left hand are featured in the following eight exercises, only the right hand version will be used in Lesson 12.

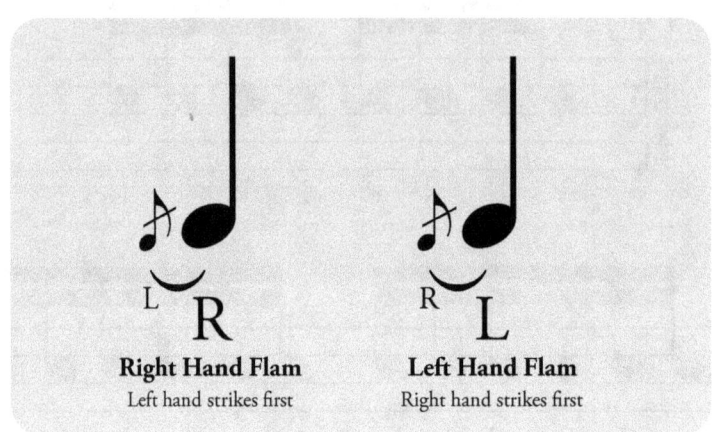

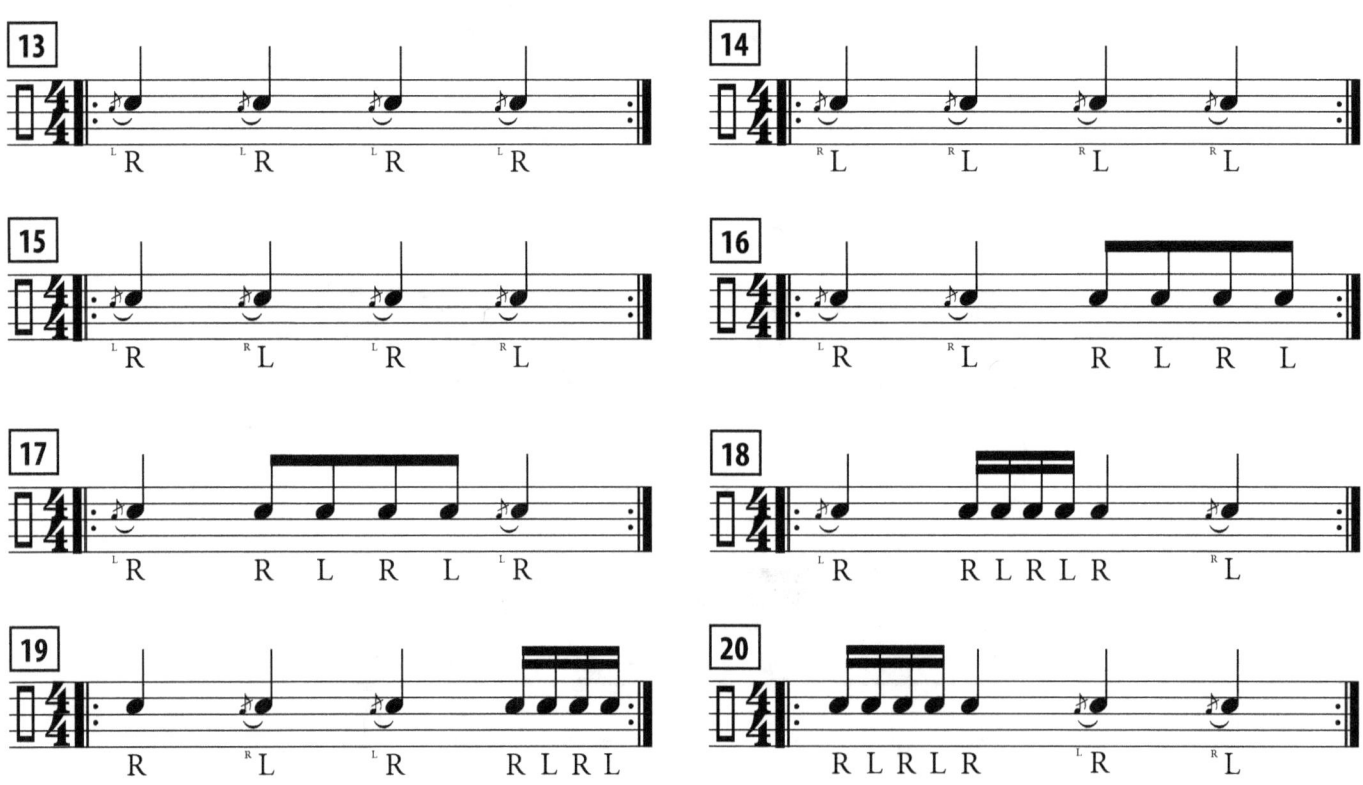

SECTION 2

Drum Set Grooves

Lessons 5 - 9

A drum set groove refers to the rhythm established by combining several drum set components together, usually the *hi-hat, snare drum* and *bass drum*. This requires the addition of the right foot, as well as assigning each hand to a different rhythm and drum set component. While the first section featured single line rhythms, we can think of this section as featuring *multiple line rhythms*.

The snare and bass patterns of this section play strictly on eighth note beats. Lessons 5 - 8 are devoted to playing these patterns while focusing on four distinct rhythms played on the hi-hat: **eighth notes, quarter notes, off-beat eighth notes** and **sixteenth notes**.

■ Common Backbeat Grooves

Drum set grooves feature a merging of several rhythms, now assigned to the right hand, the left hand, and the right foot. Merging the three rhythms seen below produces what is perhaps the most basic drum set groove in existence, often referred to as a *common backbeat groove*.

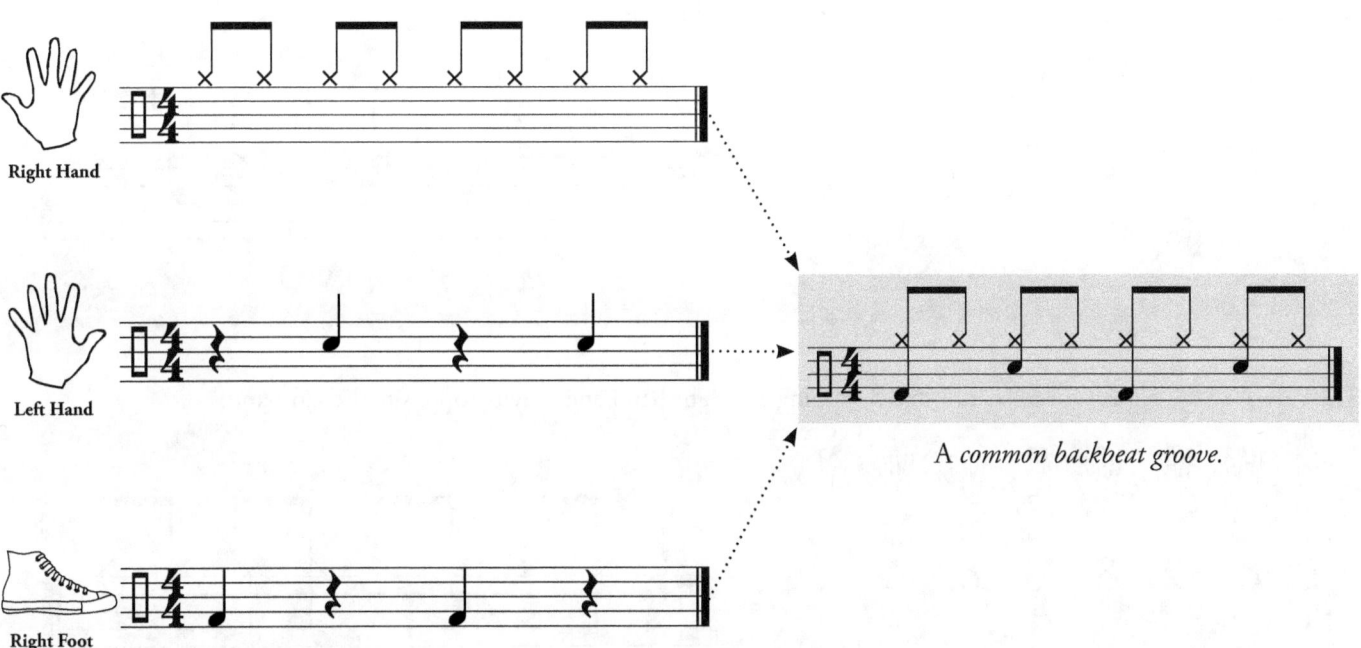

A common backbeat groove.

Section 2 | Drum Set Grooves | Lessons 5 - 9

■ Quickly Building a Common Backbeat Groove

By assigning "tasks" to each limb, a *common backbeat groove* can easily be constructed.

Right Hand
Plays on: **1 & 2 & 3 & 4 &**. The right hand should line up with every number and '&' of the spoken eighth notes.

Left Hand
Plays *with* the right hand on beats **2** and **4**.

Right Foot
Plays *with* the right hand on beats **1** and **3**.

STEP 1: Continuously count eighth notes out loud, with the **right hand** *tapping* on every spoken eighth note.

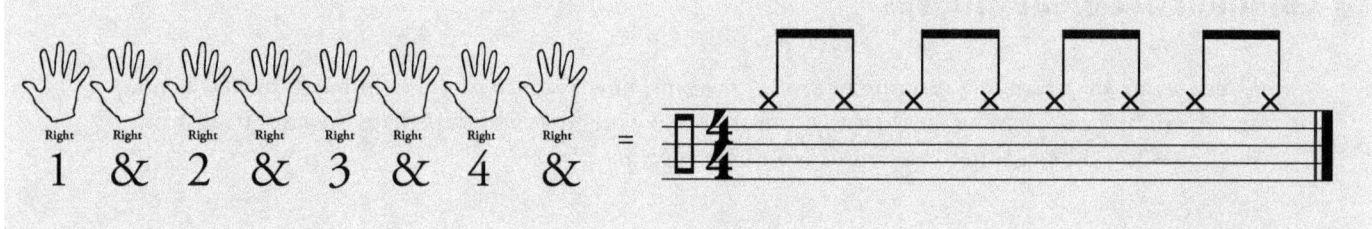

STEP 2: Add the **left hand** to beats **2** and **4**, *joining* the right hand.

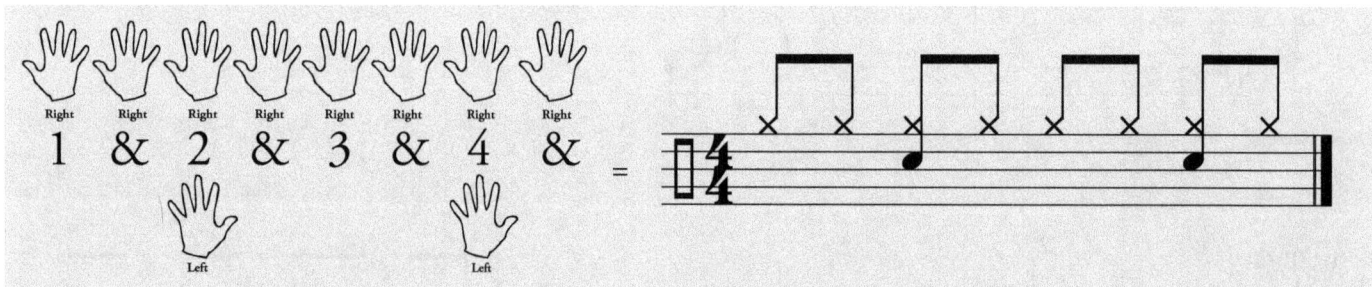

STEP 3: Add the **right foot** to beats **1** and **3**, joining the right hand and playing opposite the left hand.

Section 2 | Drum Set Grooves | *Lessons 5- 9*

◼ Section Exercises

The exercises featured in lessons 5 - 8 focus on the hi-hat playing a different rhythm for each lesson; all variation between exercises will occur within the patterns of the bass and snare.

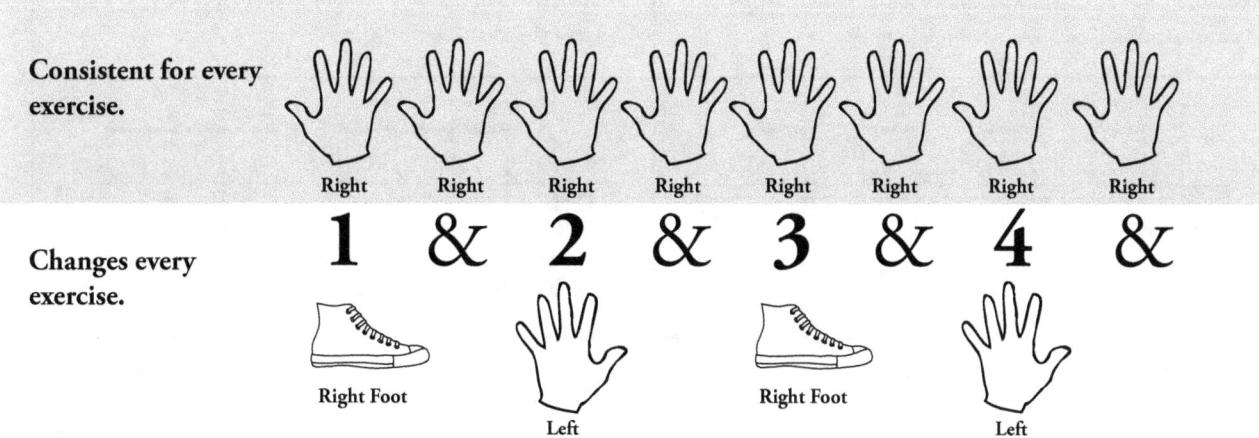

◼ Combining Exercises from Lessons 5 - 8

As lessons 5 - 8 each feature a different rhythm for the hi-hat, exercises are presented that transition between these rhythms, beginning in lesson 6. The tempo remaining the same as the transition is made from rhythm to rhythm should be carefully observed during these exercises.

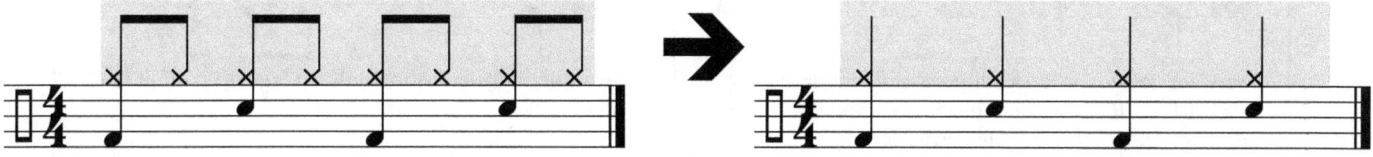

◼ Drum Set Notation

There are many ways to notate a drum set groove, and the appearance of written drum set music can often differ substantially. The following page displays different notation examples, with the same groove pattern shared between versions. The exercises of this book use the first example, defined here as *single voice notation*.

Section 2 | Drum Set Grooves | Lessons 5 - 9

Drum Set Notation Styles

Single voice notation with eighth notes grouped off in two-note batches. Used for most of this book.

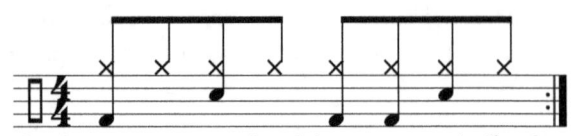

Single voice notation with eighth notes grouped off in four-note batches.

Single voice notation with eighth notes grouped off in two-note batches. Features an alternate 'X' notation.

Single voice notation with eighth notes grouped off in four-note batches. Features an alternate 'X' notation.

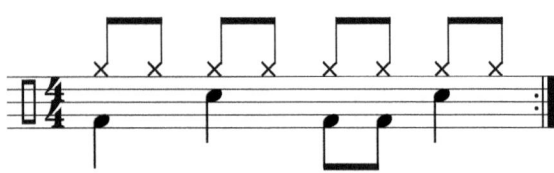

Two voice notation with eighth notes grouped in two-note batches. Notes played on the drums are notated with the stems facing down.

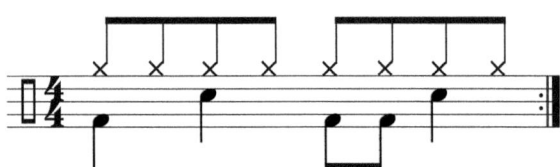

Two voice notation with eighth notes grouped in four-note batches.

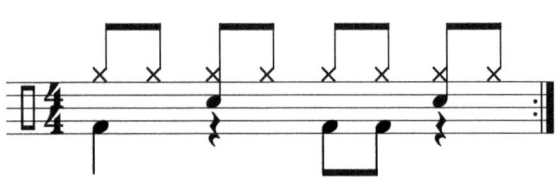

Two voice notation with eighth notes grouped off in two-note batches. The snare and hi-hat share a voice, with the bass notes written with the stems facing down.

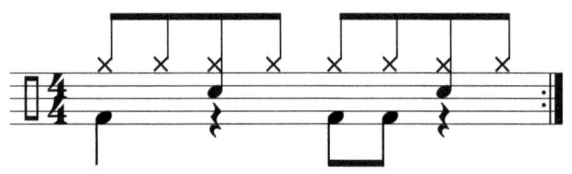

Two voice notation with eighth notes grouped off in four-note batches.

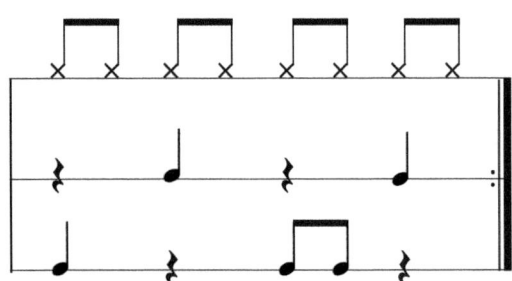

Three voice notation with eighth notes grouped off in two-note batches. Features a 'stretched' staff and usually only seen in instructional textbooks.

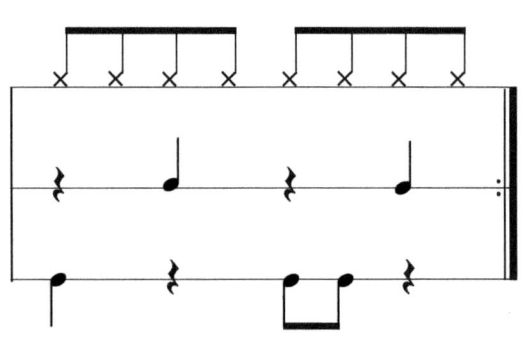

Three voice notation with eighth notes grouped off in four-note batches. In this example, the bass drum notes are written with the stems facing down.

Lesson 5
Eighth Notes on the Hi-Hat

For all exercises in this lesson, the right hand will accompany *every* note played with the left hand or right foot.

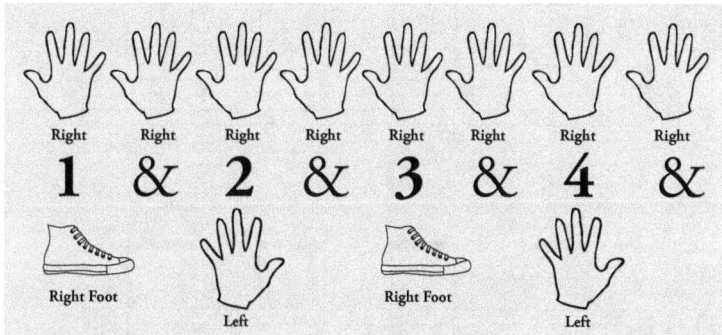

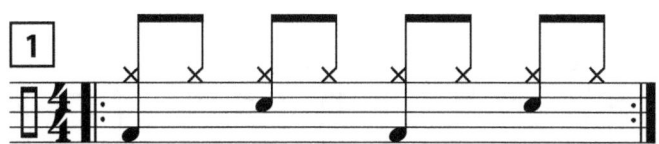

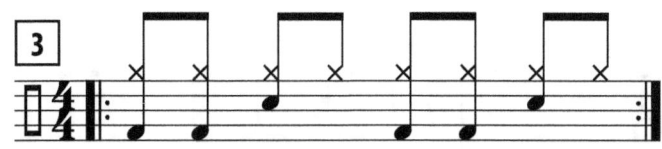

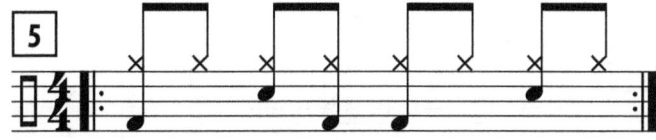

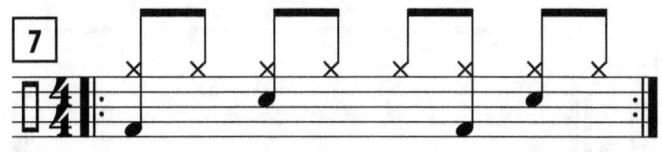

Lesson 5 | Eighth Notes on the Hi-Hat

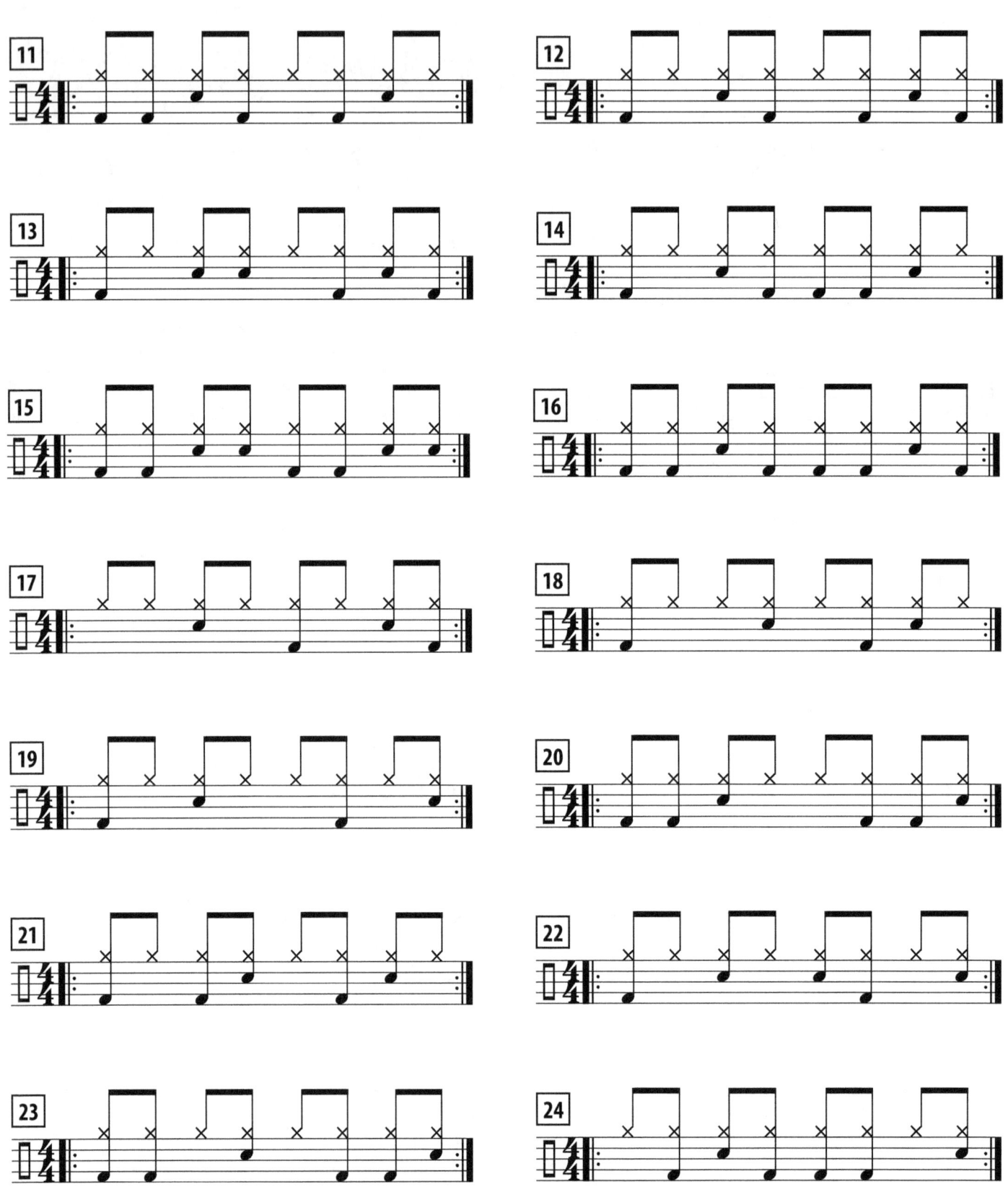

Lesson 5 | Eighth Notes on the Hi-Hat

Two Measure Phrases

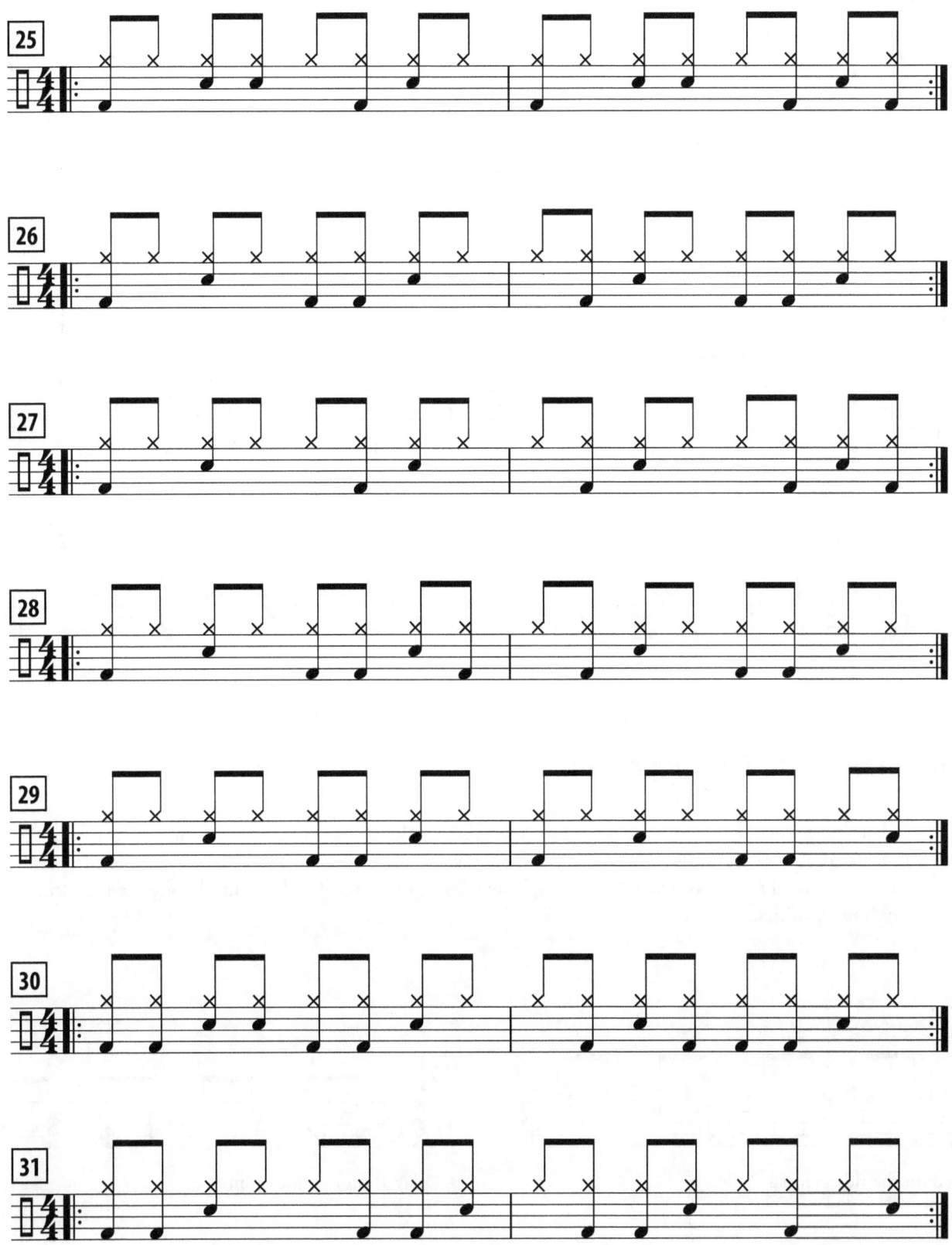

Lesson 5 | Eighth Notes on the Hi-Hat

■ Alternate Drum Set Components

Other drum set components besides the hi-hat are also frequently used to play eighth notes, such as the *floor tom* or *ride cymbal*. While the motor skills are theoretically the same between each component, the change in sound as well as position of the right-hand/arm can often *feel* different, despite the identical rhythmic qualities.

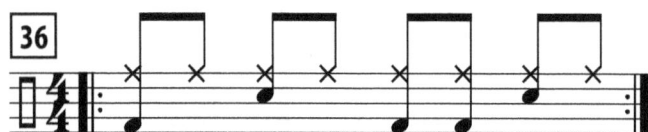

#2 played on the ride cymbal

#2 played on the floor tom

Lesson 5 | Eighth Notes on the Hi-Hat

Exercise #38 transitions to a different drum set component every two measures. Practice applying this exercise concept to other snare and bass patterns from this lesson.

"Four on the Floor"

Exercises #39 - #42 feature the bass drum playing quarter notes on every beat, often called "four on the floor." It is important that the *bass and snare properly line up on beats 2 and 4*, as seen in #40.

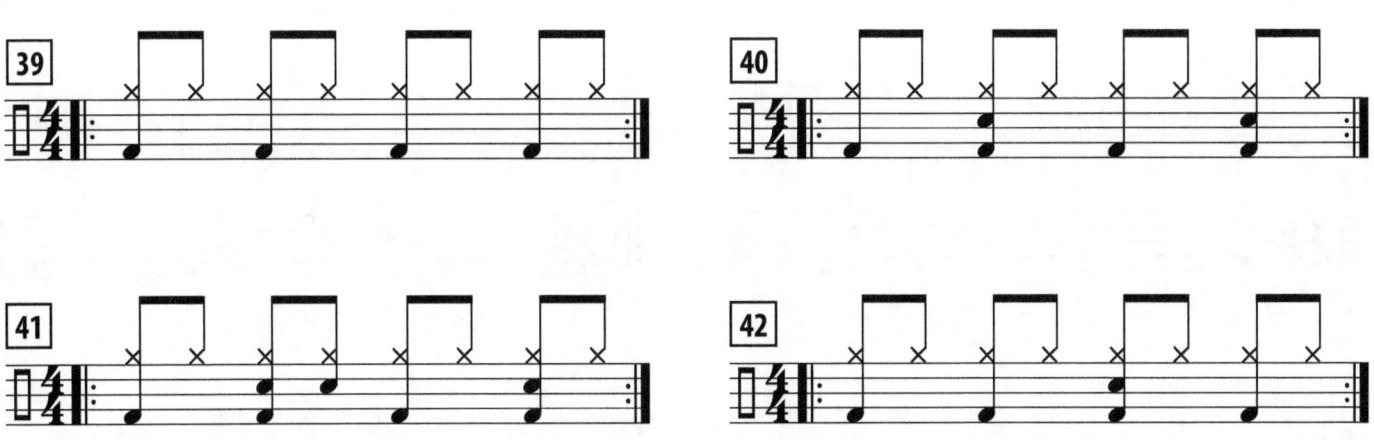

Lesson 6
Quarter Notes on the Hi-Hat

Although the right hand is only playing on the quarter note beats, it is advised that *eighth notes continue to be counted during each exercise*, with special attention paid to the bass or snare playing independently on the eighth note beats, first seen in #2 or #4.

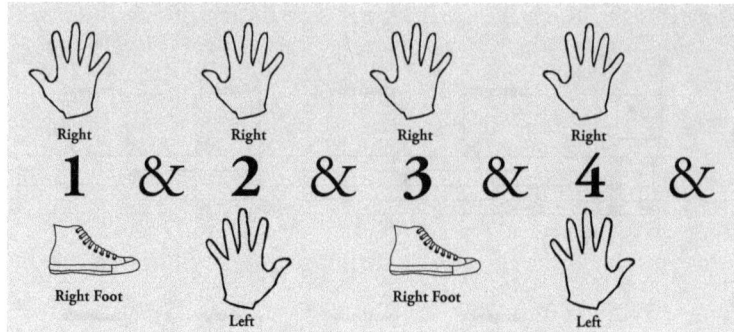

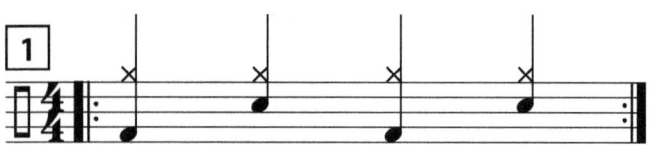

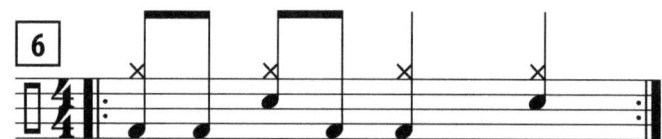

Lesson 6 | Quarter Notes on the Hi-Hat

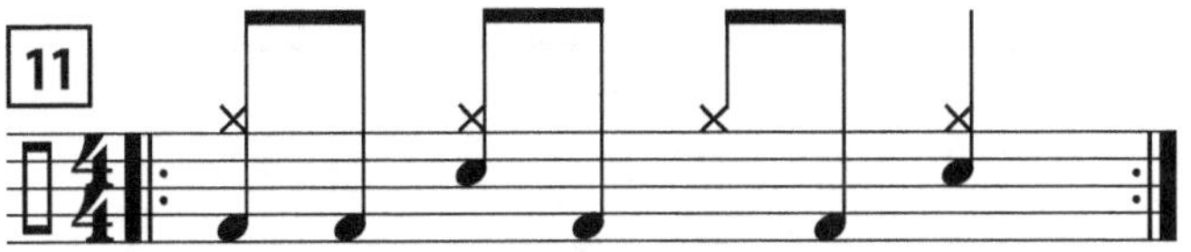

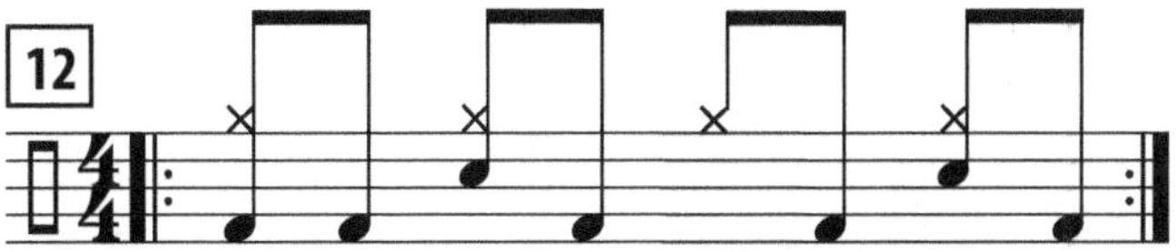

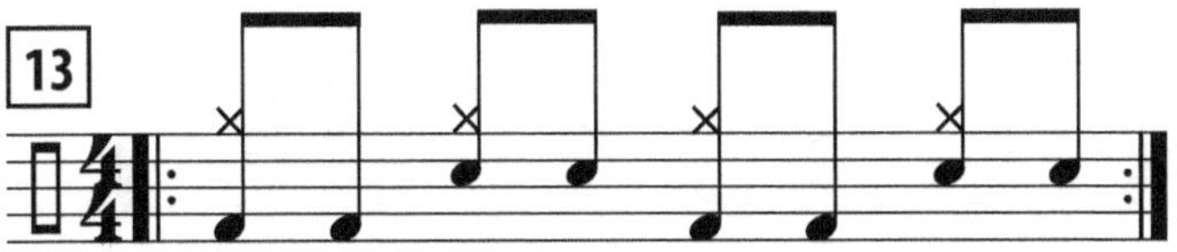

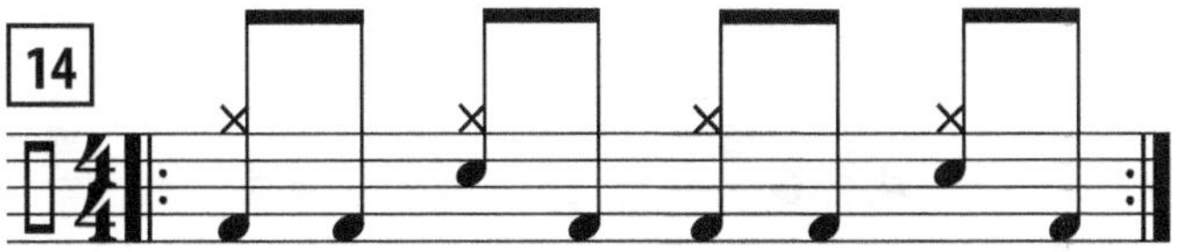

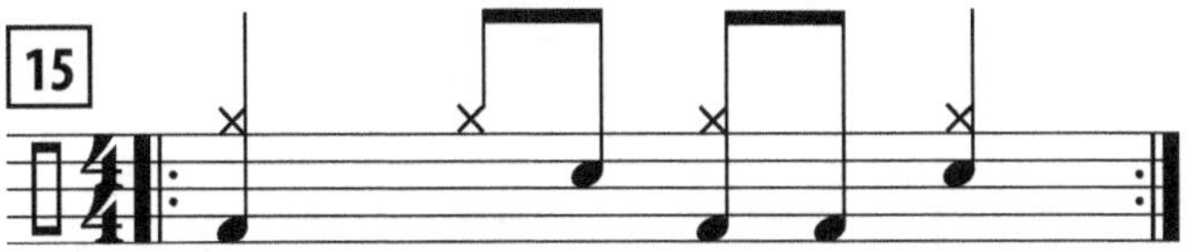

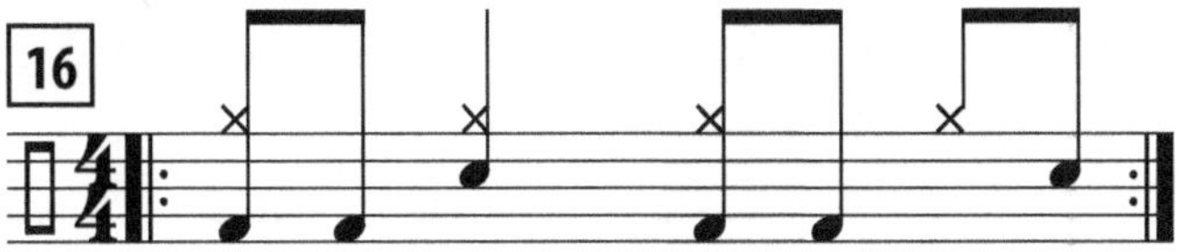

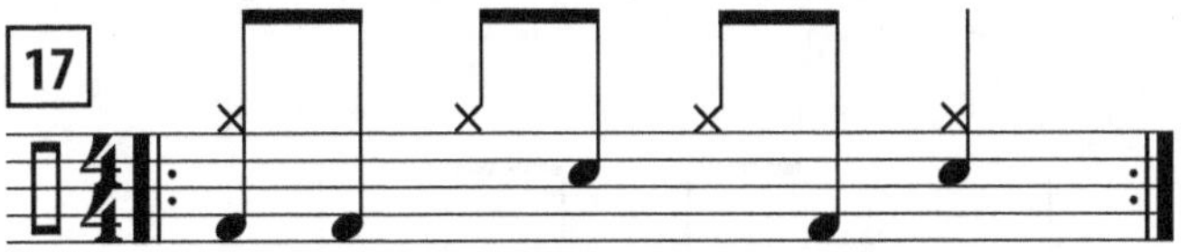

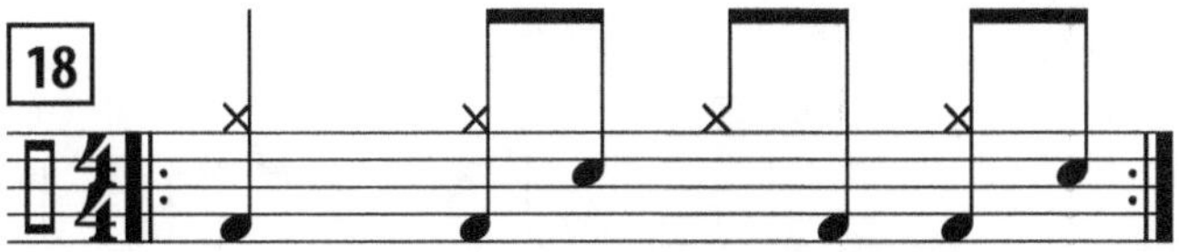

Combining with Eighth Notes

Exercises #19 - #22 precede grooves from this lesson with their eighth note counterpart from Lesson 5. The goal should be to *remain consistent with the tempo as the transition is made every two measures*.

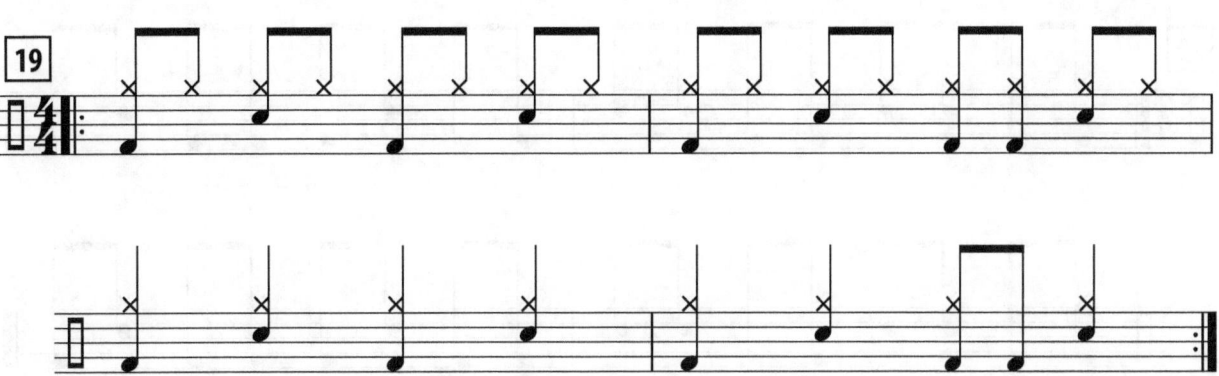

Lesson 6 | Quarter Notes on the Hi-Hat

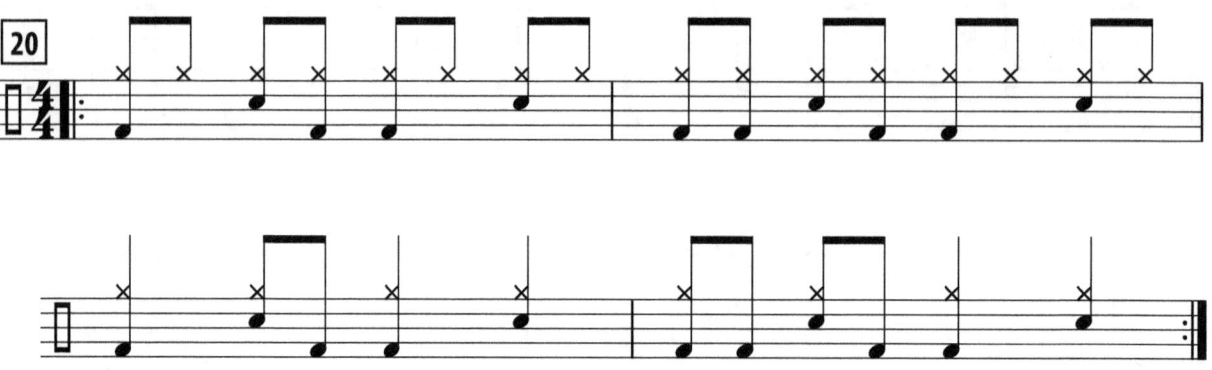

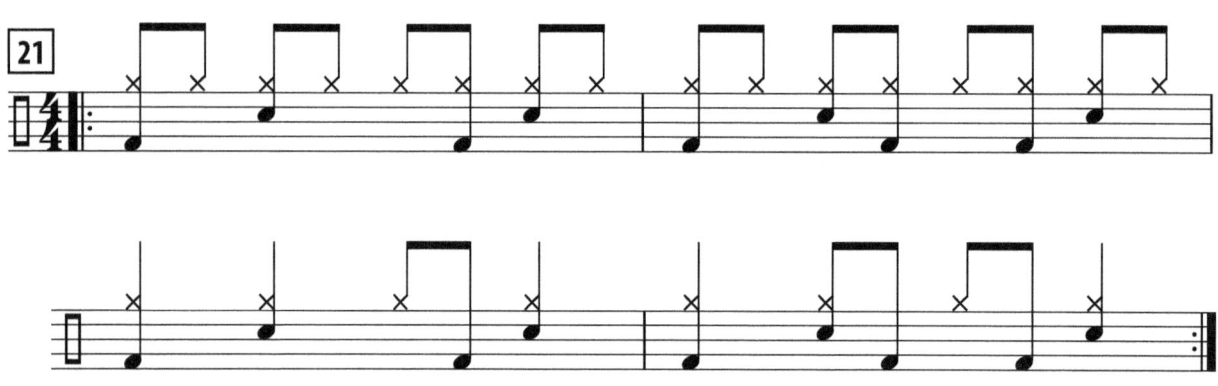

Lesson 7

Off-Beat Eighth Notes on the Hi-Hat

Exercise #1 from this lesson introduces a **linear groove**, defined as a groove in which no two beats are played at the same time. Notice that #2 - #10 are *not* linear, as the bass or snare begin to join the right hand on the off-beats.

1

2

3

4

5

6

7

8

9

10

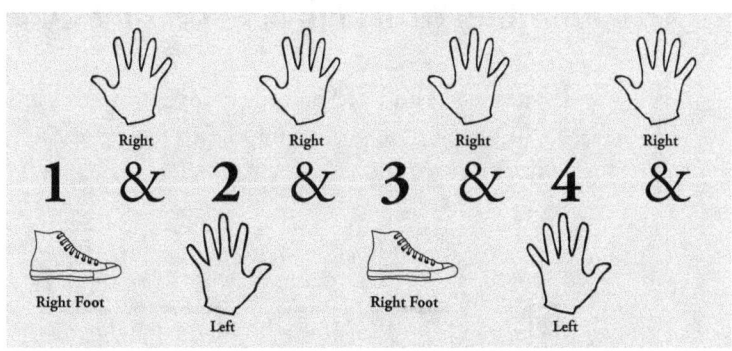

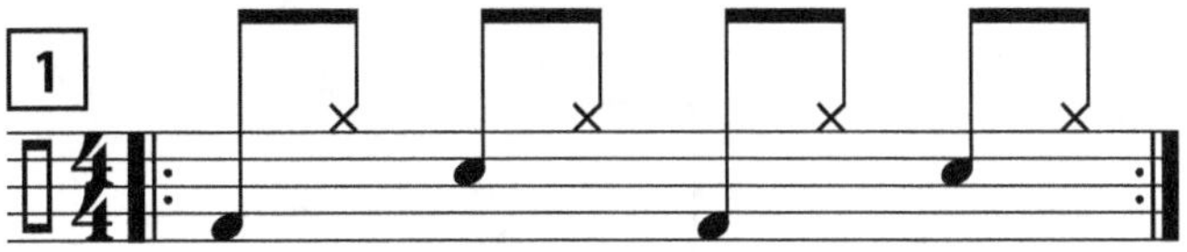

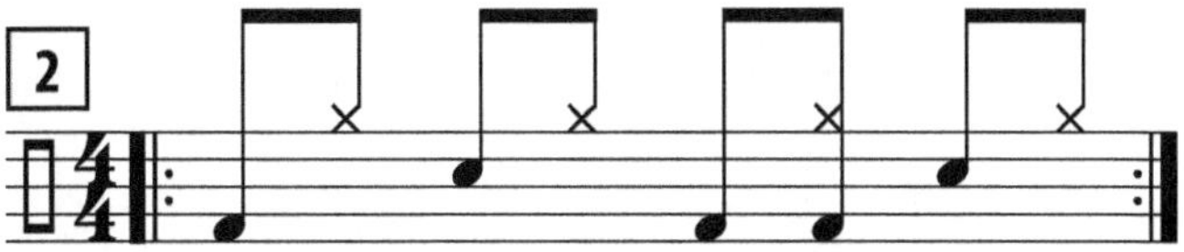

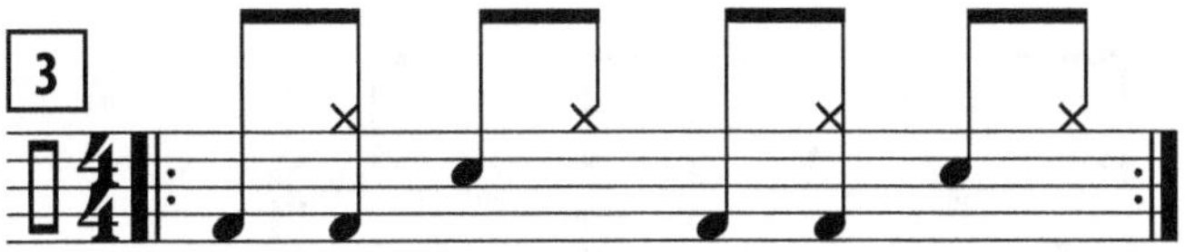

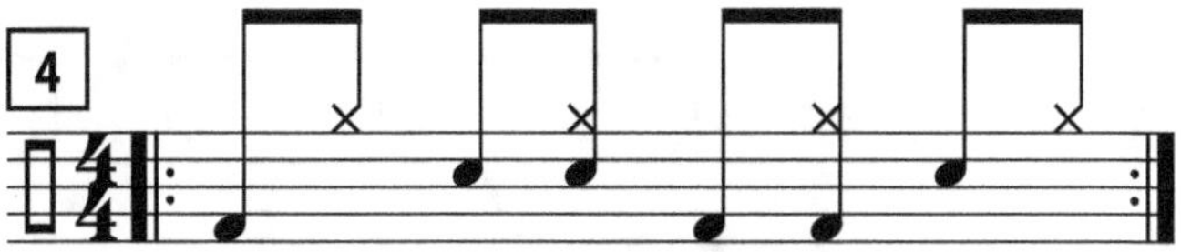

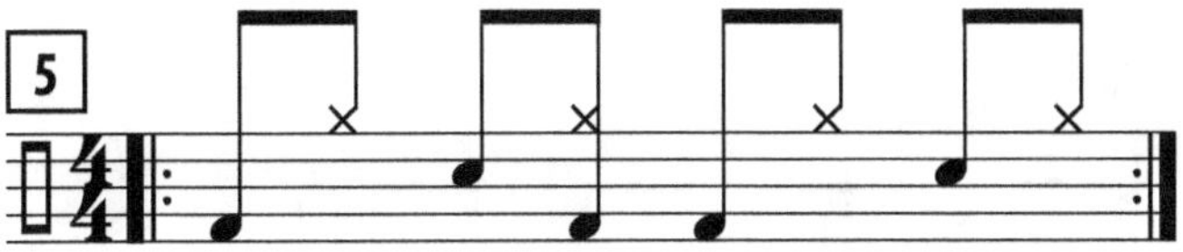

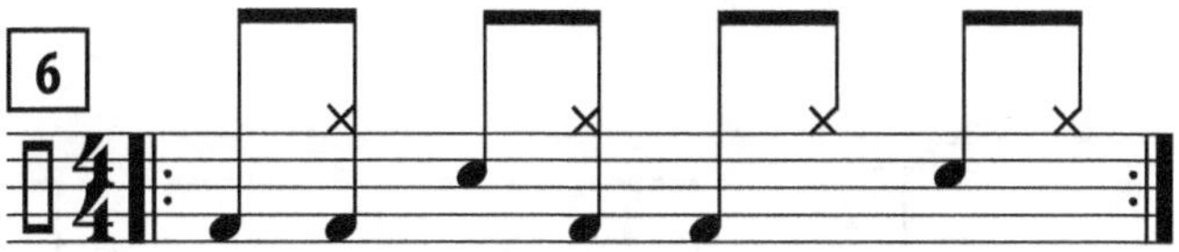

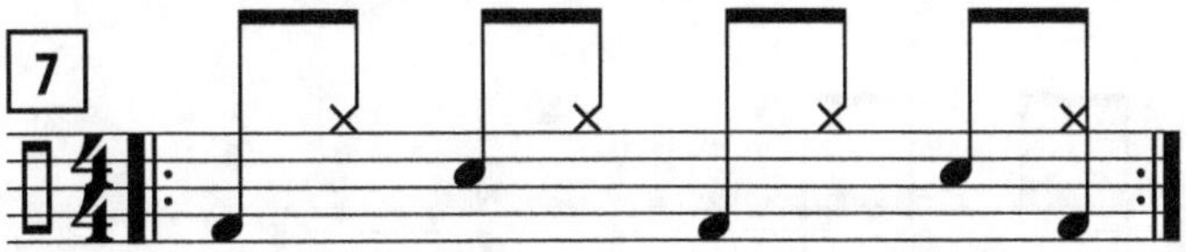

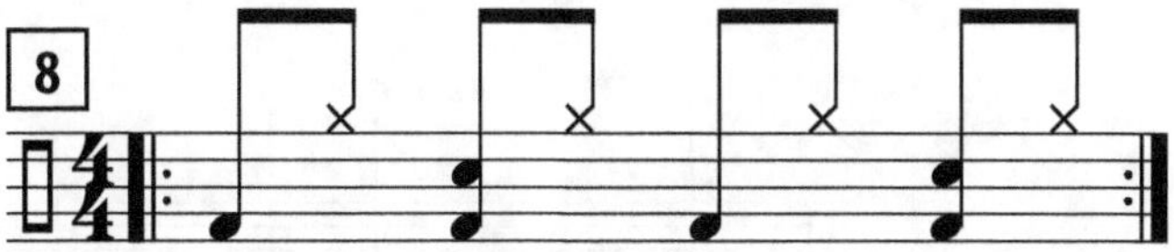

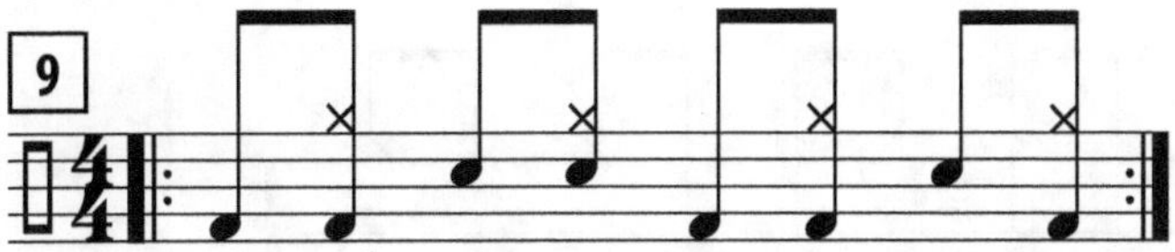

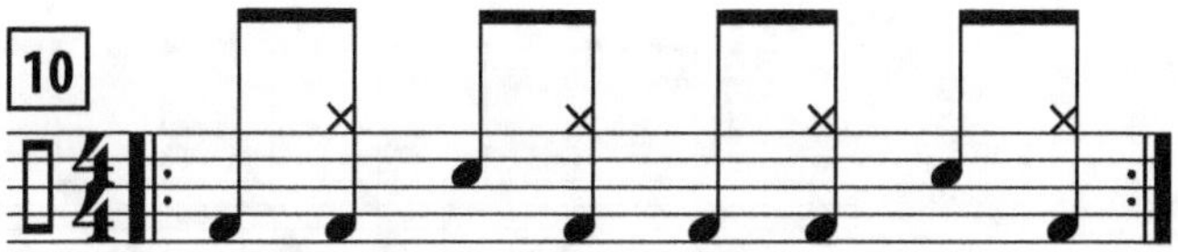

Lesson 7 | Off-Beat Eighth Notes on the Hi-Hat

■ Combining with Eighth Notes and Quarter Notes

Exercises #11 and #12 precede grooves from this lesson with their counterpart from Lesson 5 and Lesson 6. As always, the goal should be to *remain consistent with the tempo as the transition is made every two measures.*

Lesson 8
Sixteenth Notes on the Hi-Hat

The sixteenth note grooves featured in this lesson are intended to be initially played with *alternate sticking*, implying that both hands will play a single stroke sticking pattern on the hi-hat, with the right hand *moving* to the snare on beats 2 and 4. When played this way, these grooves are the only grooves in this book that feature the right hand playing the snare drum, with the left hand staying on the hi-hat for the duration of the groove.

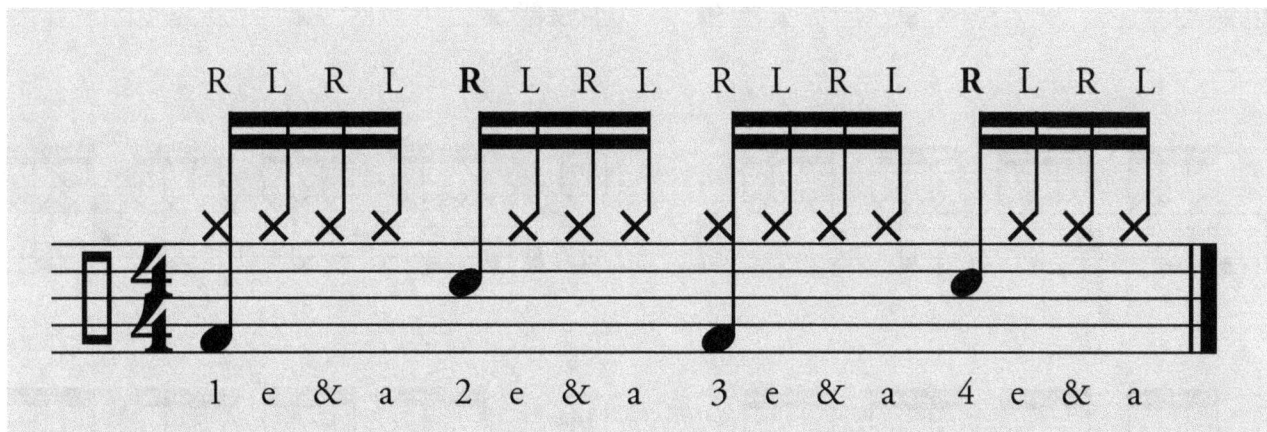

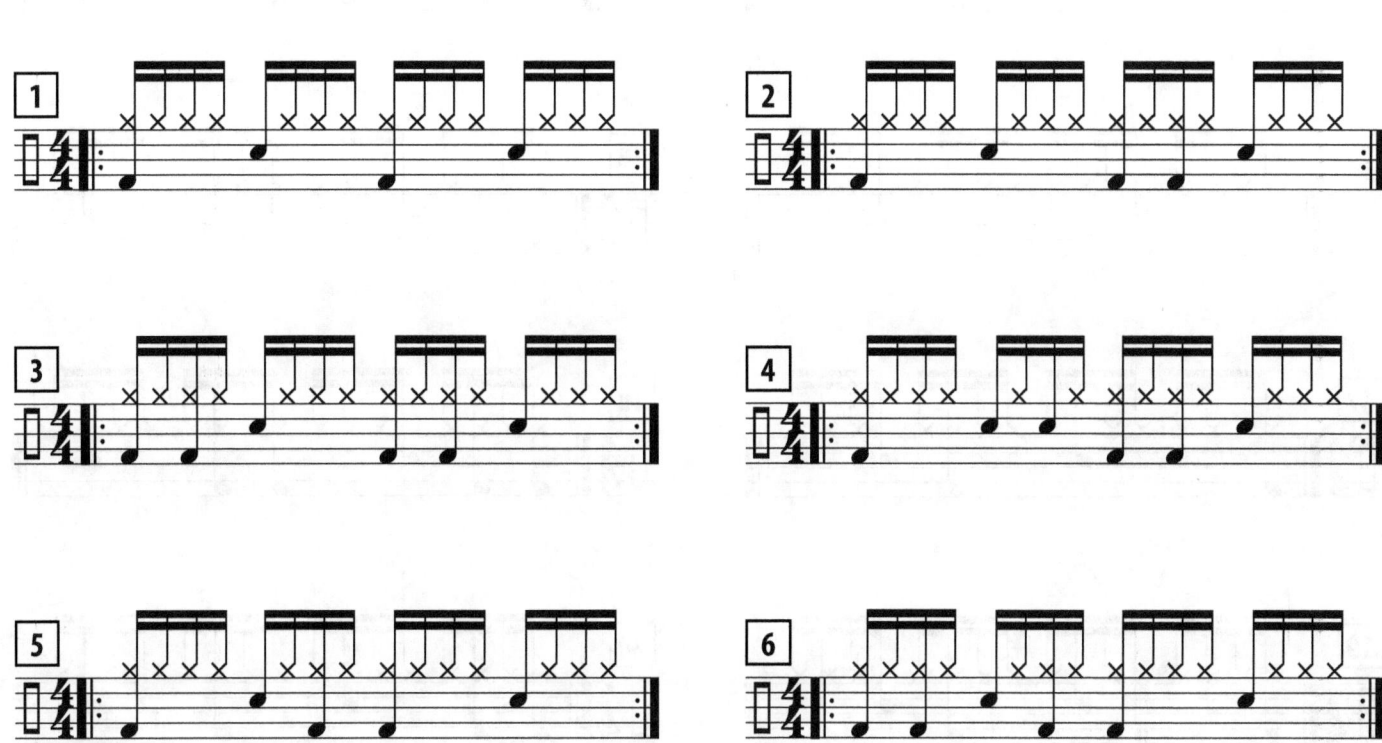

Lesson 8 | Sixteenth Notes on the Hi-Hat

42

Lesson 8 | Sixteenth Notes on the Hi-Hat

■ Single-Handed Sticking

While it is recommended that alternate sticking be practiced first, the previous eighteen exercises can be optionally played *single-handed*, which will feature the right hand playing all sixteenth note beats and the left hand playing the snare back-beats, similar to grooves from lessons 5-7. While exercises #21 and #22 demonstrate this concept, this sticking pattern can be applied to all previous sixteenth note exercises from this lesson.

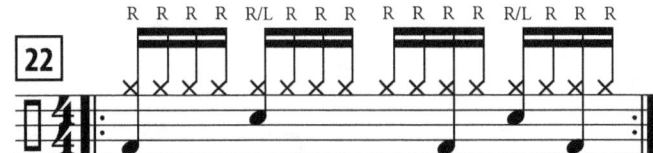

■ The *Journey Through The Rhythms* Exercise

Exercises #23 - #29 transition between all four hi-hat rhythms, creating an exercise concept called *Journey Through The Rhythms*. The ability to comfortably transition from rhythm to rhythm without changing the tempo or pausing between lines should be carefully observed.

Lesson 8 | Sixteenth Notes on the Hi-Hat

Lesson 8 | Sixteenth Notes on the Hi-Hat

■ *Journey Through The Rhythms* with Transitioning Components

Exercise #26 revists the bass and snare patterns of #23, now with a different drum set component assigned to each rhythm.

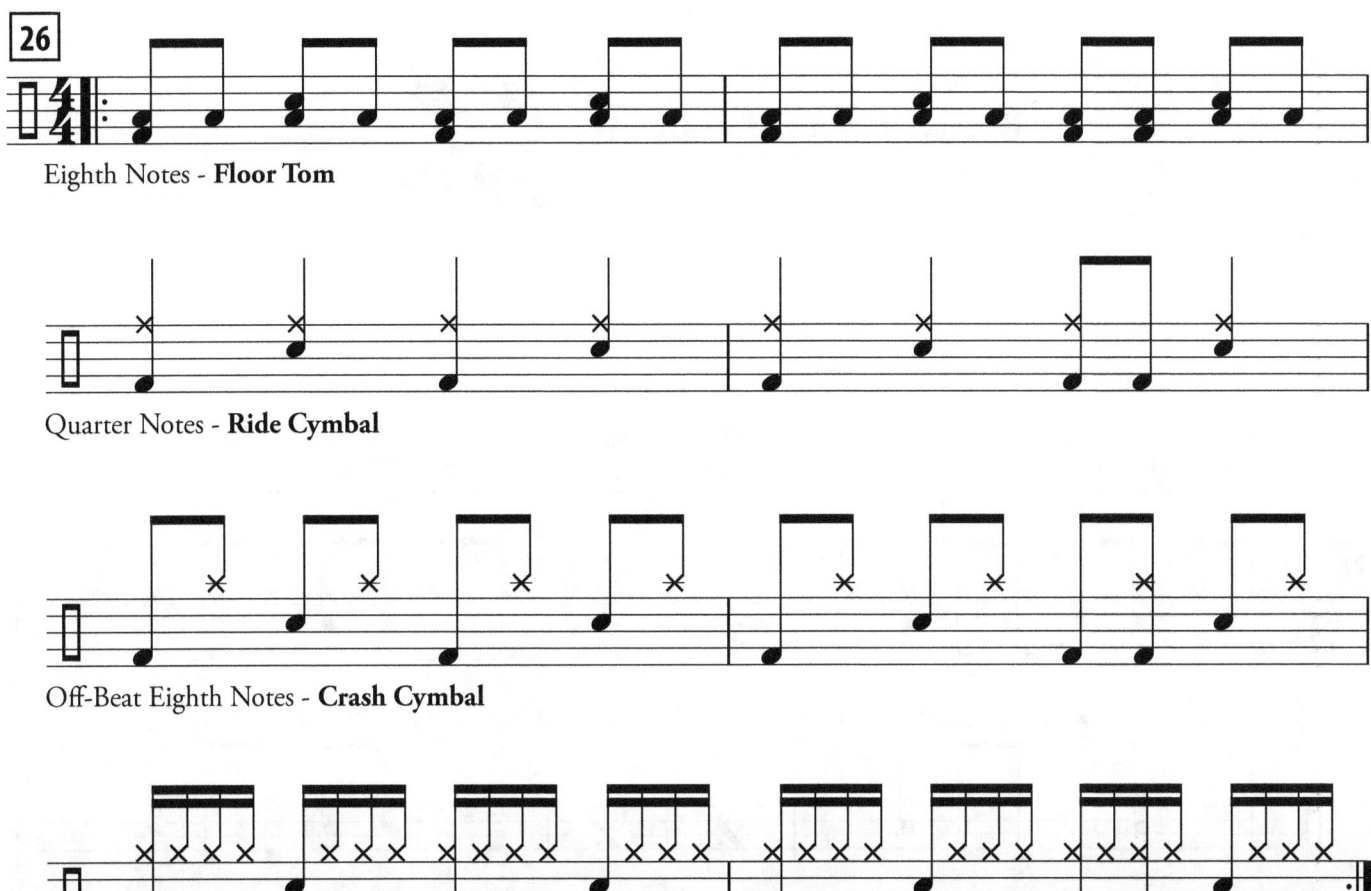

Eighth Notes - **Floor Tom**

Quarter Notes - **Ride Cymbal**

Off-Beat Eighth Notes - **Crash Cymbal**

Sixteenth Notes - **Hi Hat**

Lesson 8 | Sixteenth Notes on the Hi-Hat

■ *Journey Through The Rhythms* with Repeating Measures

Exercises #27 - #29 utilize a *repeat previous measure* symbol, which will lengthen the *Journey Through The Rhythms* exercise to sixteen measures, with the transition to a new hi-hat rhythm now occuring every four measures. Notice that each line features three measures of the same bass and snare pattern, followed by one measure of an alternate pattern.

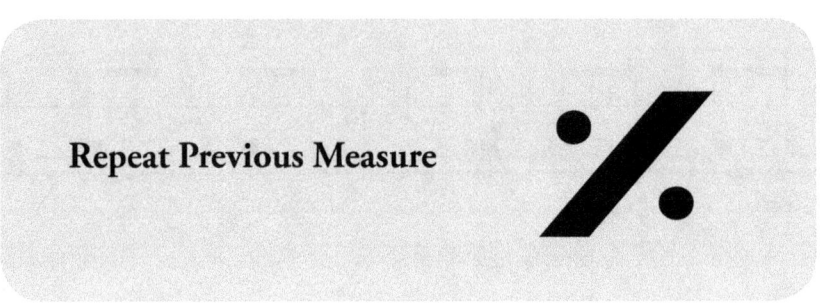

Repeat Previous Measure

46

Lesson 8 | Sixteenth Notes on the Hi-Hat

Exercise #29 features a different drum set component assigned to each rhythm.

47

Lesson 9
Rhythmic Feel Variations

A rhythmic feel refers to the consistent placement of the snare drum within a measure. Up to this point, this section has exclusively featured *common backbeat grooves*, in which the snare plays on or around beats 2 and 4. This lesson will explore other common locations for the snare drum to be consistently played within a measure.

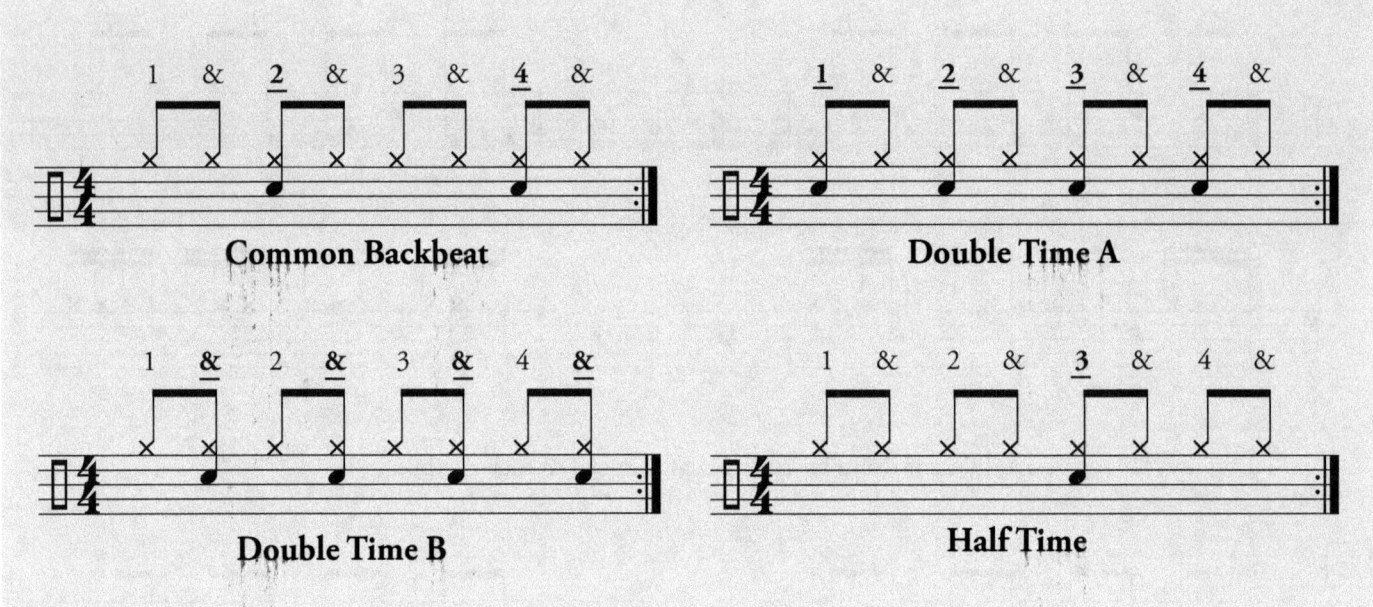

Double Time A

Double time A features the snare placed on every beat or *number* of a counted measure.

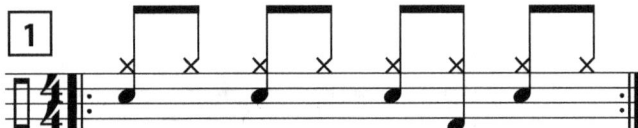   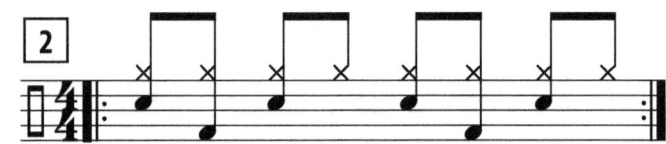

Lesson 9 | Rhythmic Feel Variations

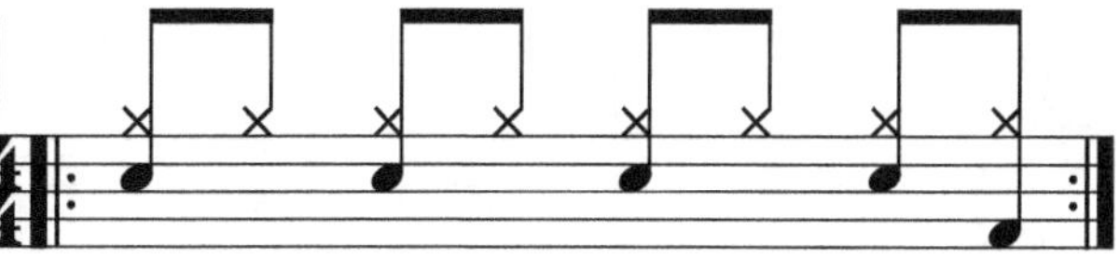

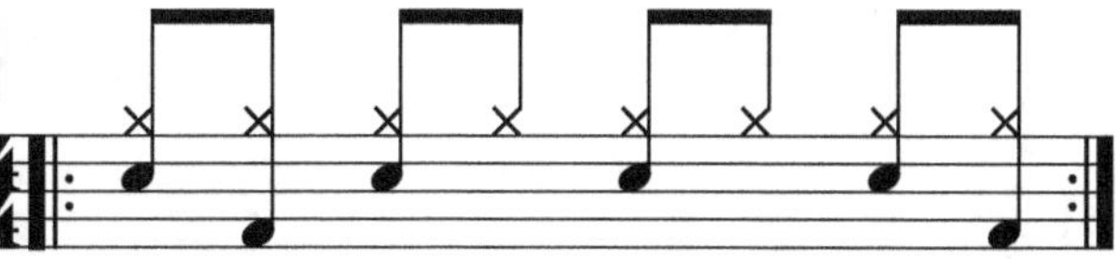

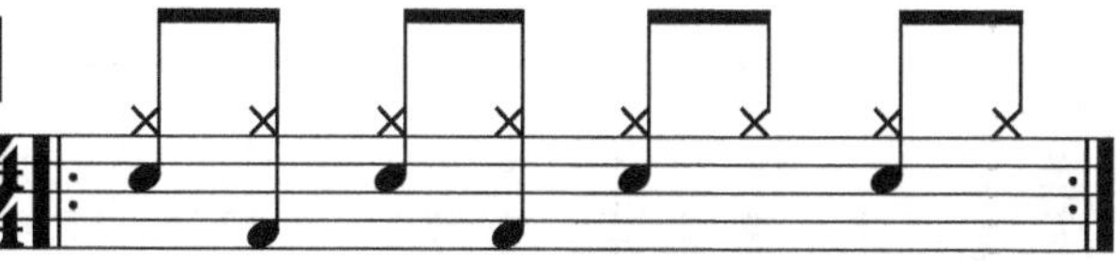

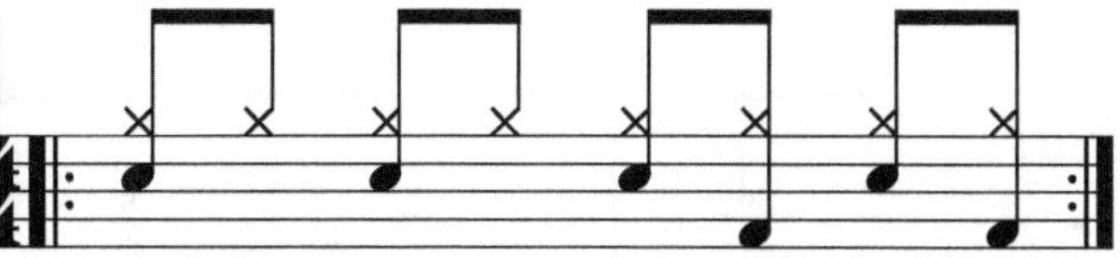

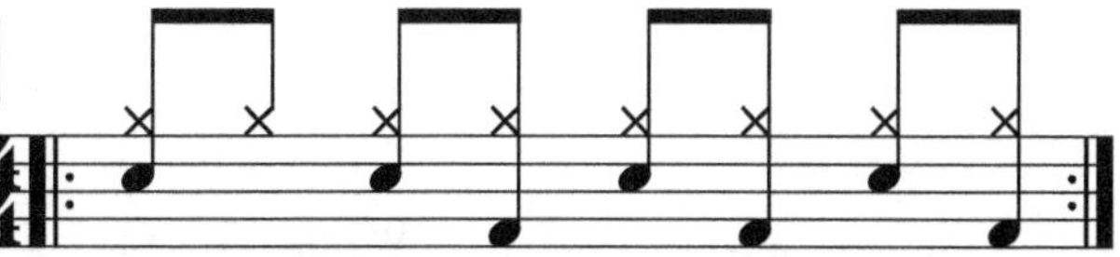

[Exercises 3–10: notated drum patterns in 4/4]

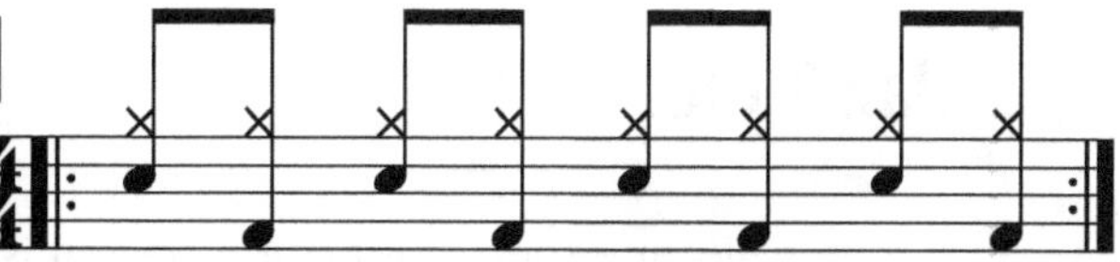

Double Time B

Double time B shifts to the off-beat, designating the snare to play on every '&' of a counted measure.

[Exercises 11–14: notated drum patterns in 4/4]

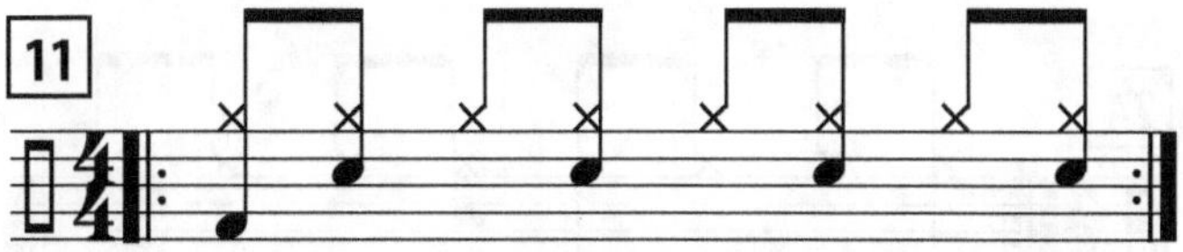

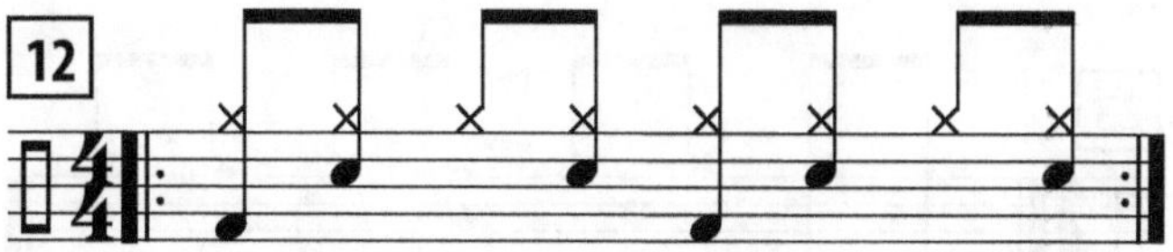

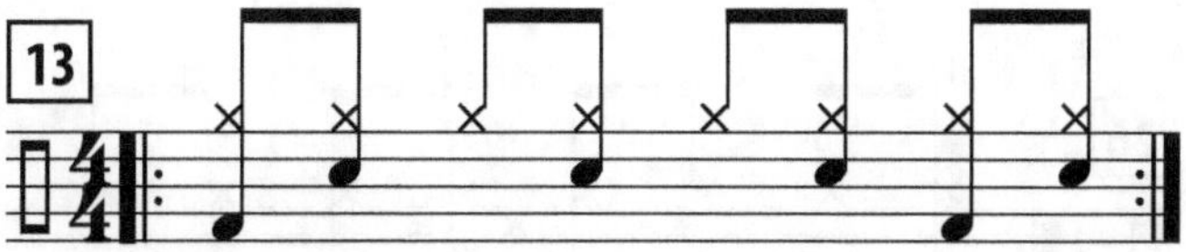

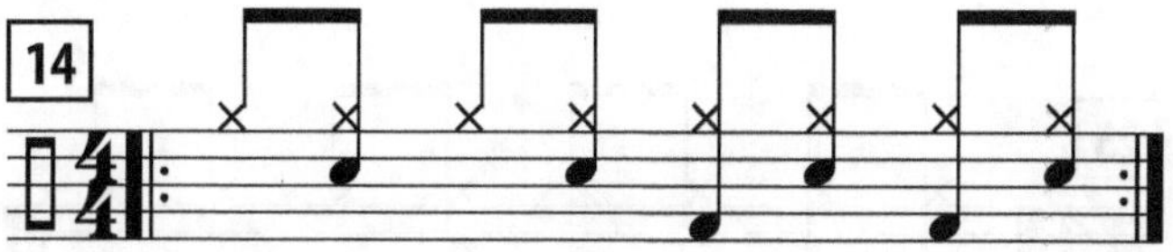

Lesson 9 | Rhythmic Feel Variations

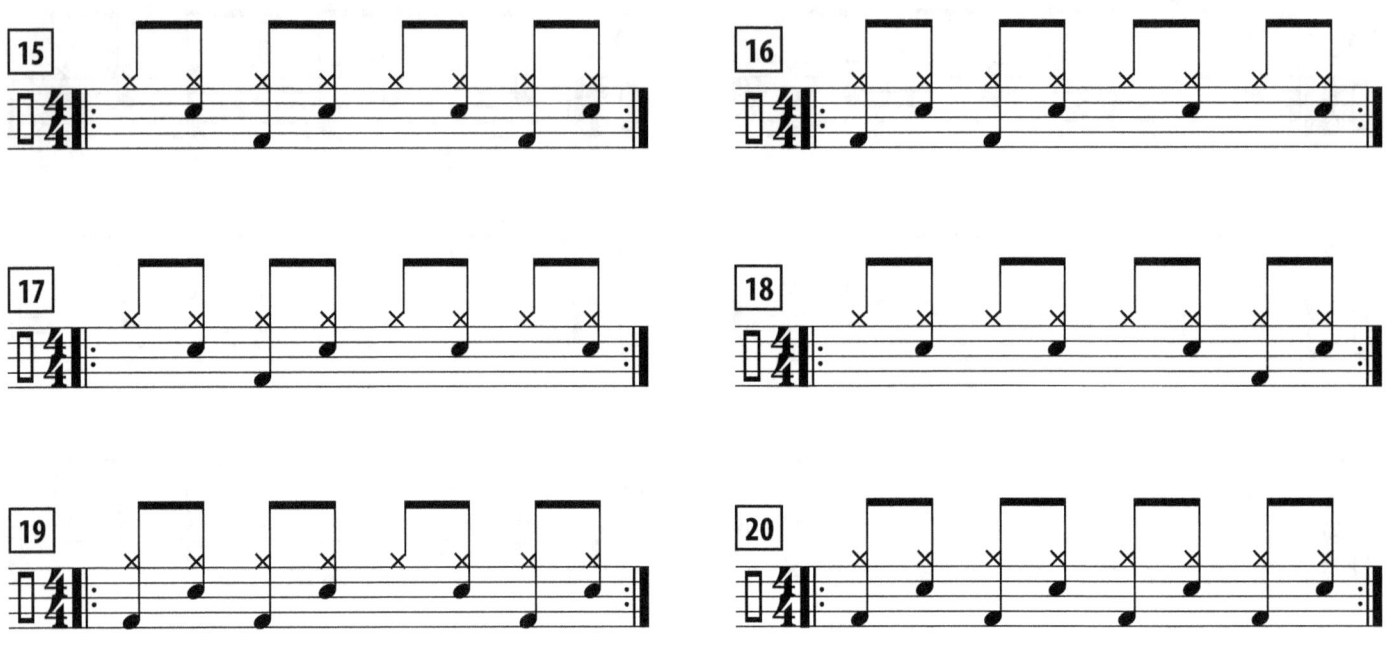

■ Half Time

A half time groove features a snare that is only playing on a single beat of the measure. While beat 3 is the most common location for the snare in a half time feel, exercises #35 - #40 place the snare on beat 4, which is a common variation.

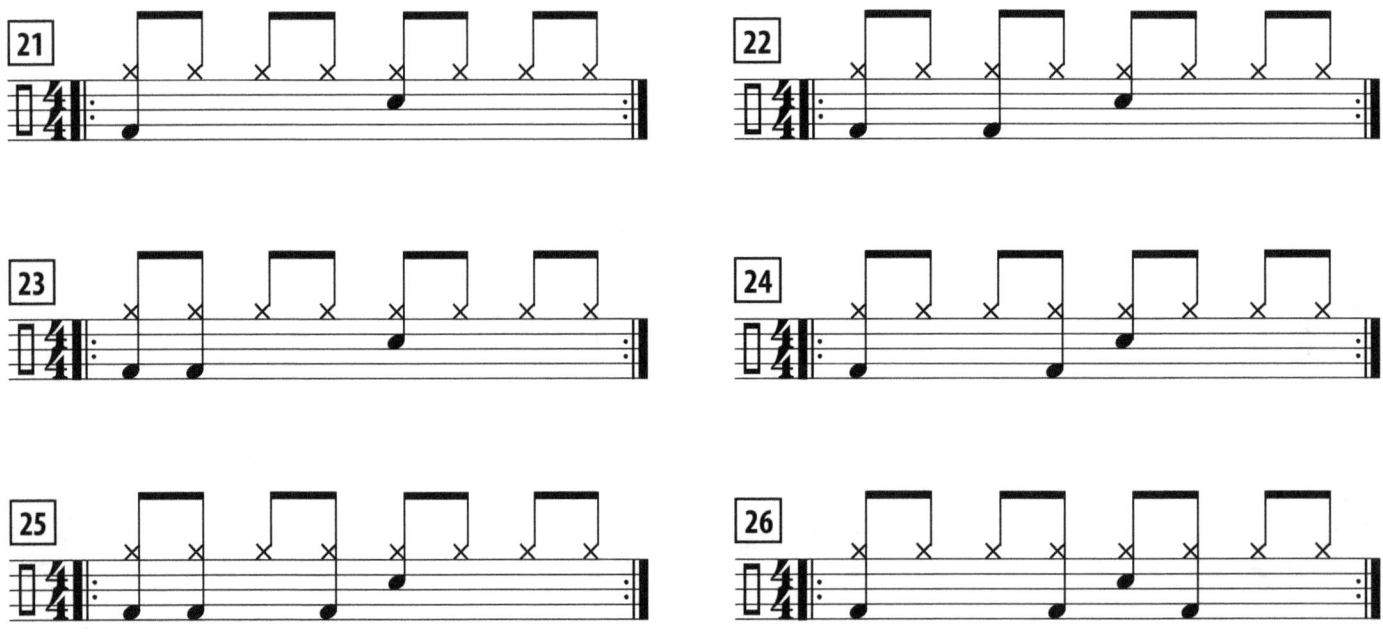

Lesson 9 | Rhythmic Feel Variations

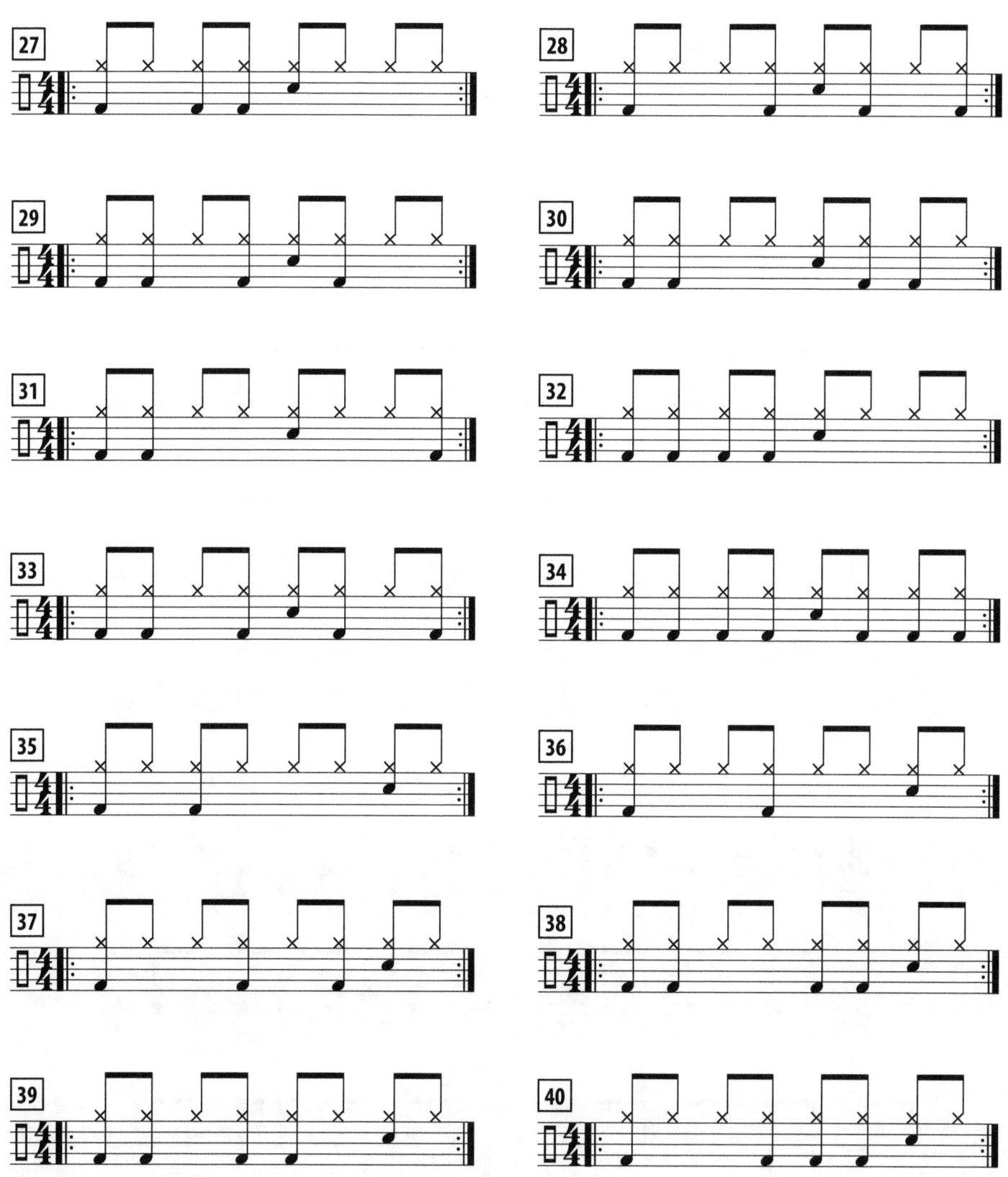

51

Lesson 9 | Rhythmic Feel Variations

Exercises #41 and #42 feature a transition between all four rhythmic feels. Each line is to be played twice.

SECTION 3: Accessories

Lessons 10 - 12

This section contains enhancements and modifications to the grooves featured in Section 2, and will call upon skills learned in all previous lessons of this book. While fully completing the first two sections is not necessary to begin this section, previously given exercises should be reviewed and reinforced as needed.

Drum Set Staff Revisited

Memorizing the drum set staff below will become increasingly useful in this section, as almost every type of drum set notation is used and combined.

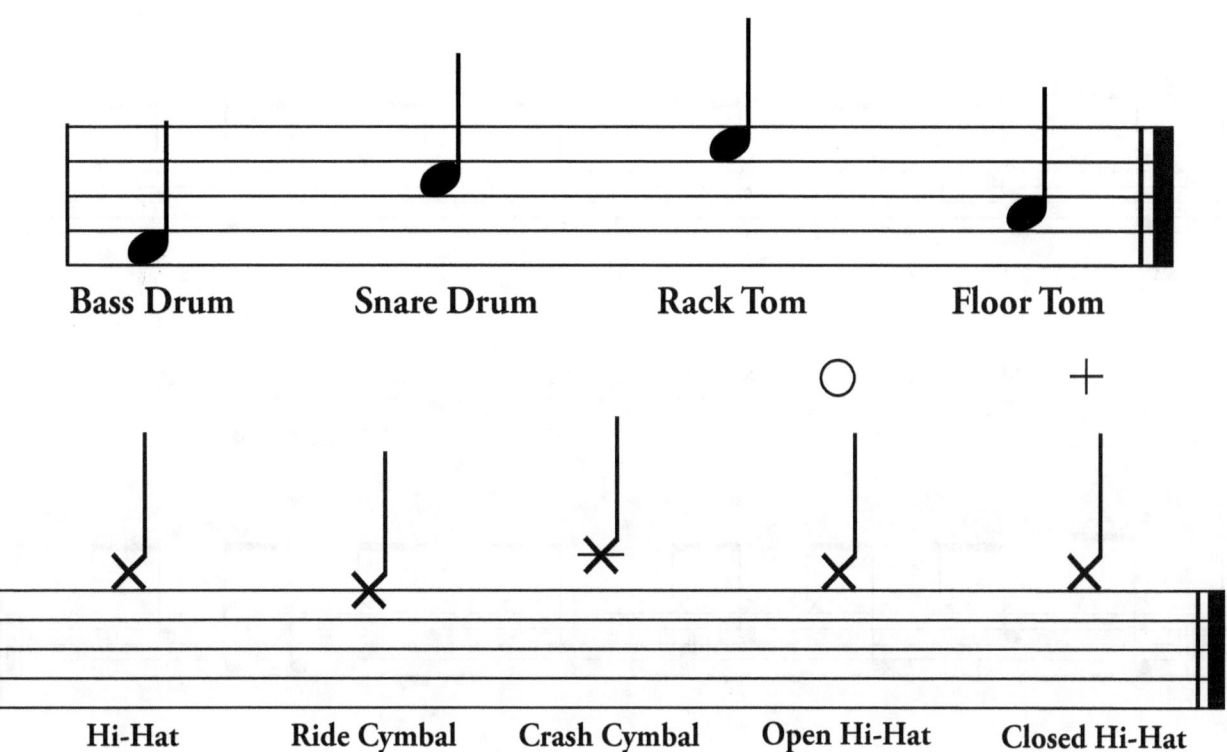

Lesson 10
Playing the Crash Cymbal

This lesson will assign the right hand to play the crash cymbal on various beats of a measure, notated here as the first ledger line above the five-line staff.

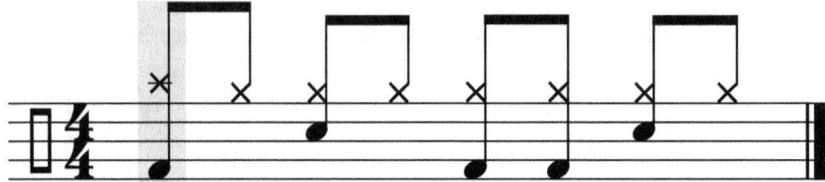

Beat 1 of the groove being replaced with a crash cymbal, seen here as the next line above the hi-hat.

Crashing on Beat 1

Exercises #1-#4 feature a crash cymbal on beat 1, using the four hi-hat rhythms from Section 2. Notice that on #4, *alternate sticking* is presented, signifying that the crash will be played with the right hand while the left hand immediately plays the following hi-hat note.

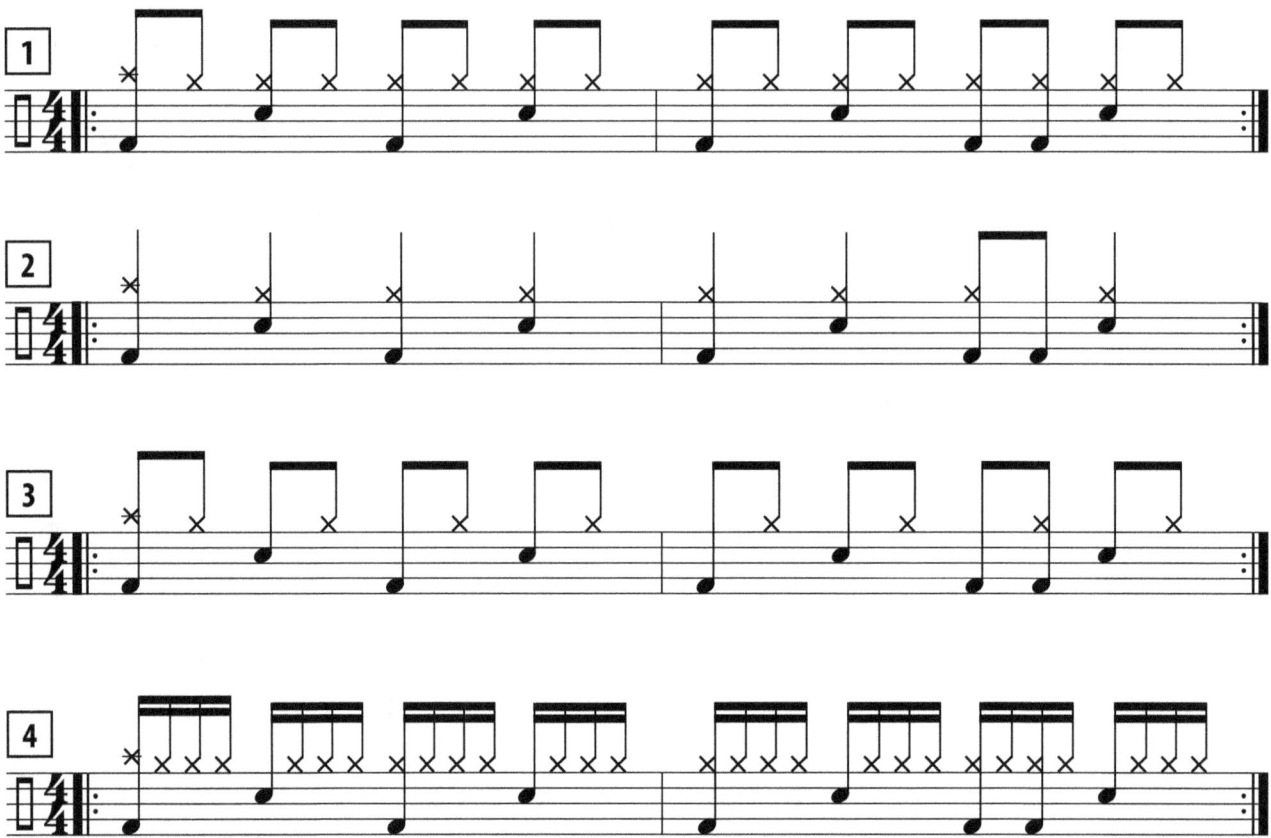

54

Lesson 10 | Playing the Crash Cymbal

■ Crashing Beyond Beat 1

The crash cymbal can also be used to accentuate certain beats within a drum groove. The following six exercises feature crashes placed on various beats of a measure, often playing alongside a snare drum note, as first seen in #5.

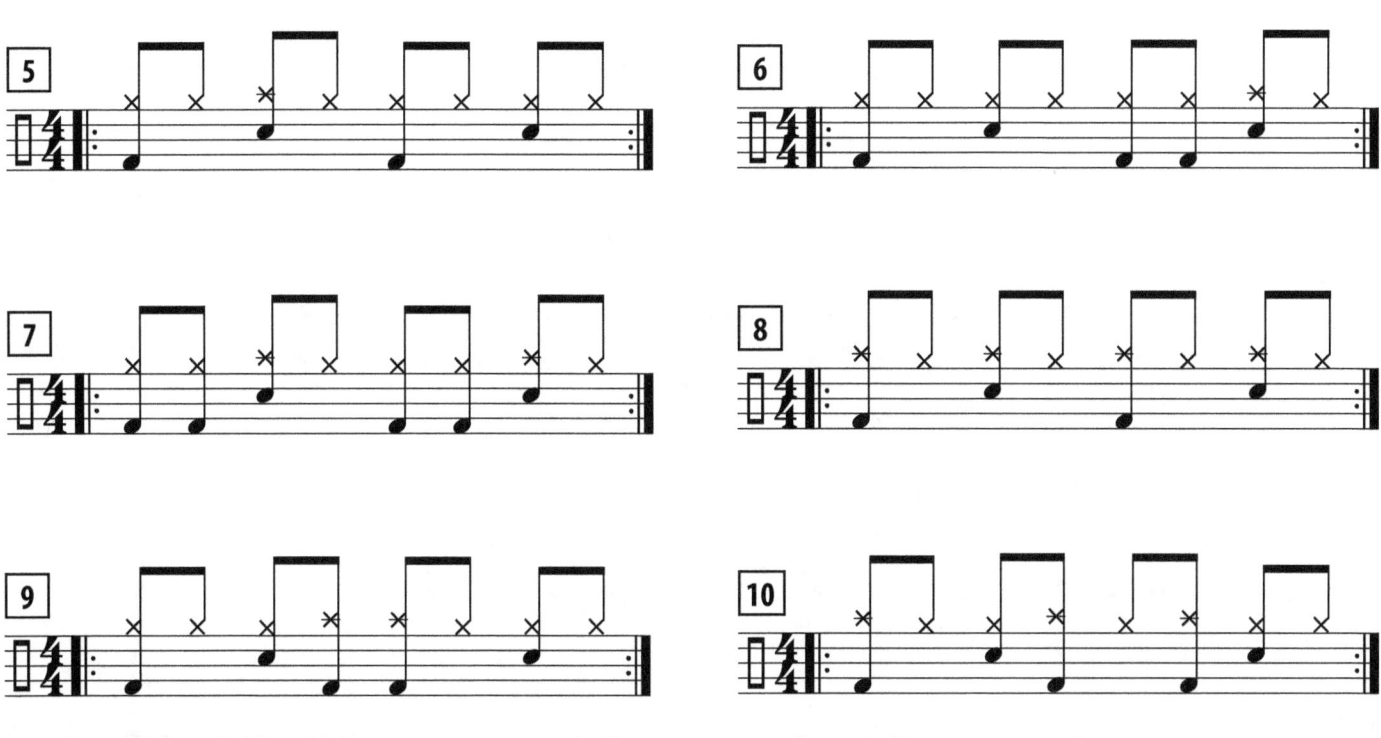

■ Riding the Crash

Exercise #11 features the crash cymbal on every beat, often referred to as **riding the crash** or **crash riding.** This concept is further explored in #12 - #14, which feature a crash cymbal played on every *quarter note* or *off-beat eighth note*.

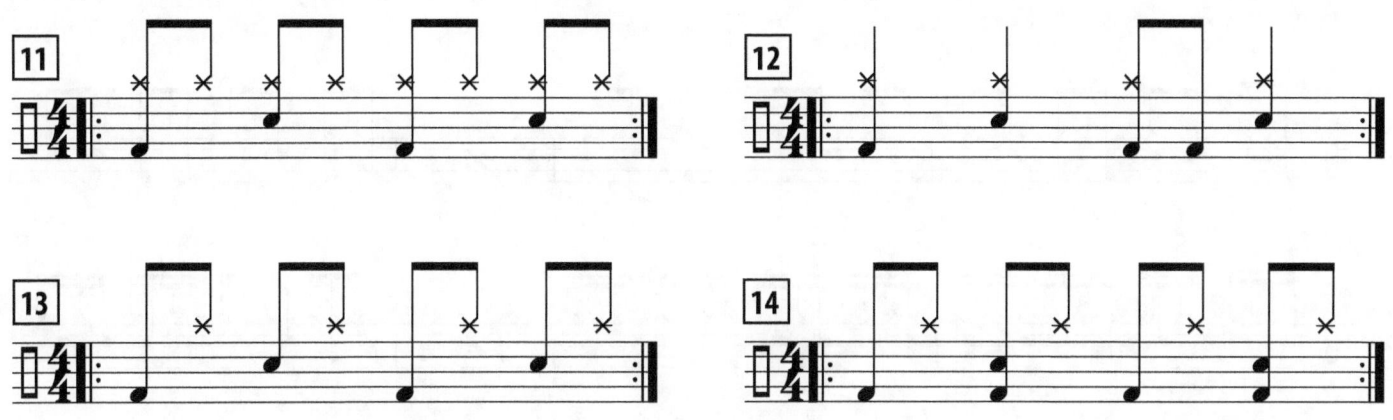

Lesson 10 | Playing the Crash Cymbal

Exercises #15 and #16 revist the *Journey Through The Rhythms* concepts from Lesson 8, now with a crash cymbal marking the transition from rhythm to rhythm.

Lesson 11
Opening the Hi-Hat

Opening the hi-hat refers to separating the top and bottom hi-hat cymbals by releasing pressure with the left foot. The hi-hat struck in this open position gives off a different sound, and is choked immediately after the strike by reapplying pressure. In this lesson, the hi-hats will be remaining open for the length of one eighth note. The symbol for opening is notated as an '**O**' above the hi-hat notes, and the close sign is notated as a '**+**'.

Opening on the '& of 2' and the '& of 4'

When the hi-hat opens on the '& of 4' or the '& of 2', it will often close alongside a bass drum note, either on beat 1 or beat 3. It is easy then to think that *both feet will strike together following the opening of the hi-hat* for many of the following exercises.

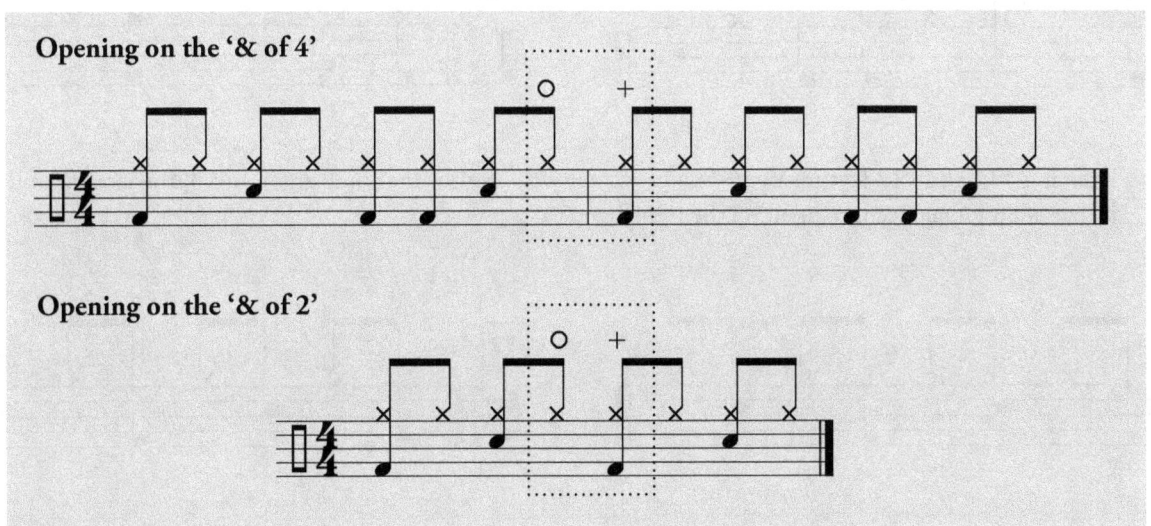

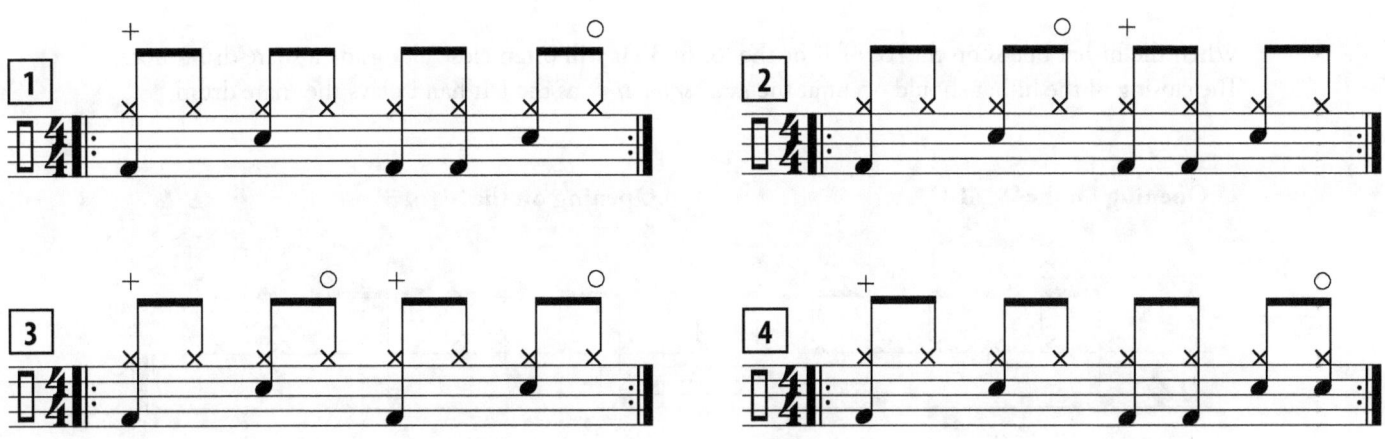

Lesson 11 | Opening the Hi-Hat

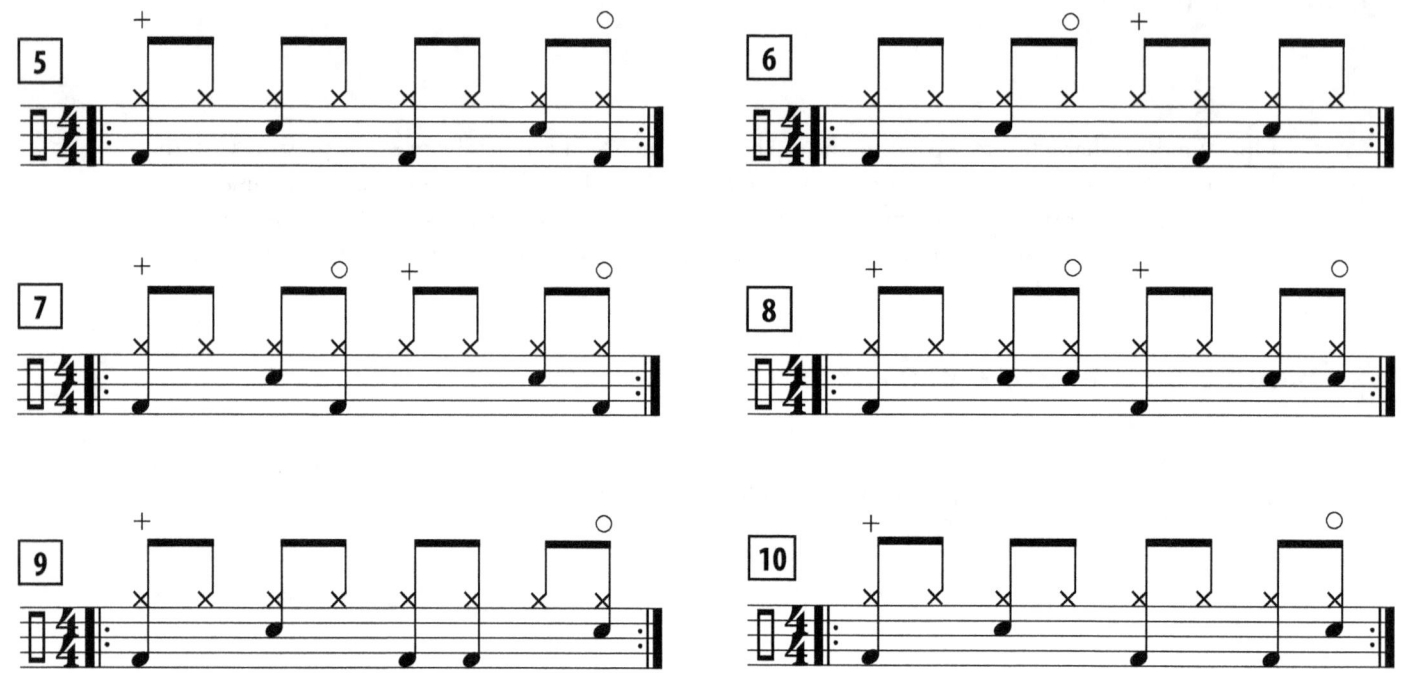

Exercises #11 and #12 feature an *off-beat hi-hat rhythm*. Notice that on beats 1 and 3, the closing of the hi-hat is no longer accompanied by the right hand.

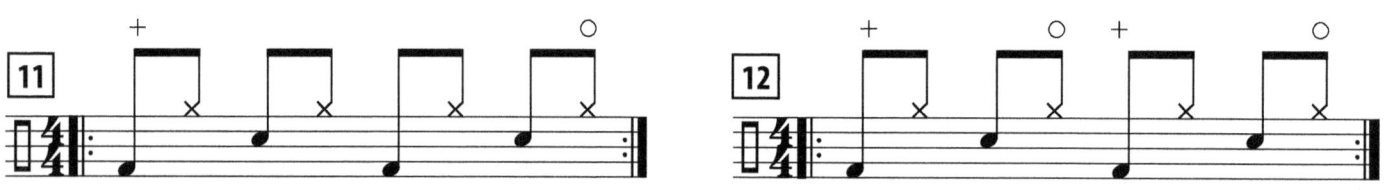

▪ Opening on the '& of 1' and the '& of 3'

When the hi-hat opens on the '& of 1' or the '& of 3', it will often close alongside a snare drum note. The closing of the hi-hat should occur at the *exact same time* as the left hand plays the snare drum.

Lesson 11 | Opening the Hi-Hat

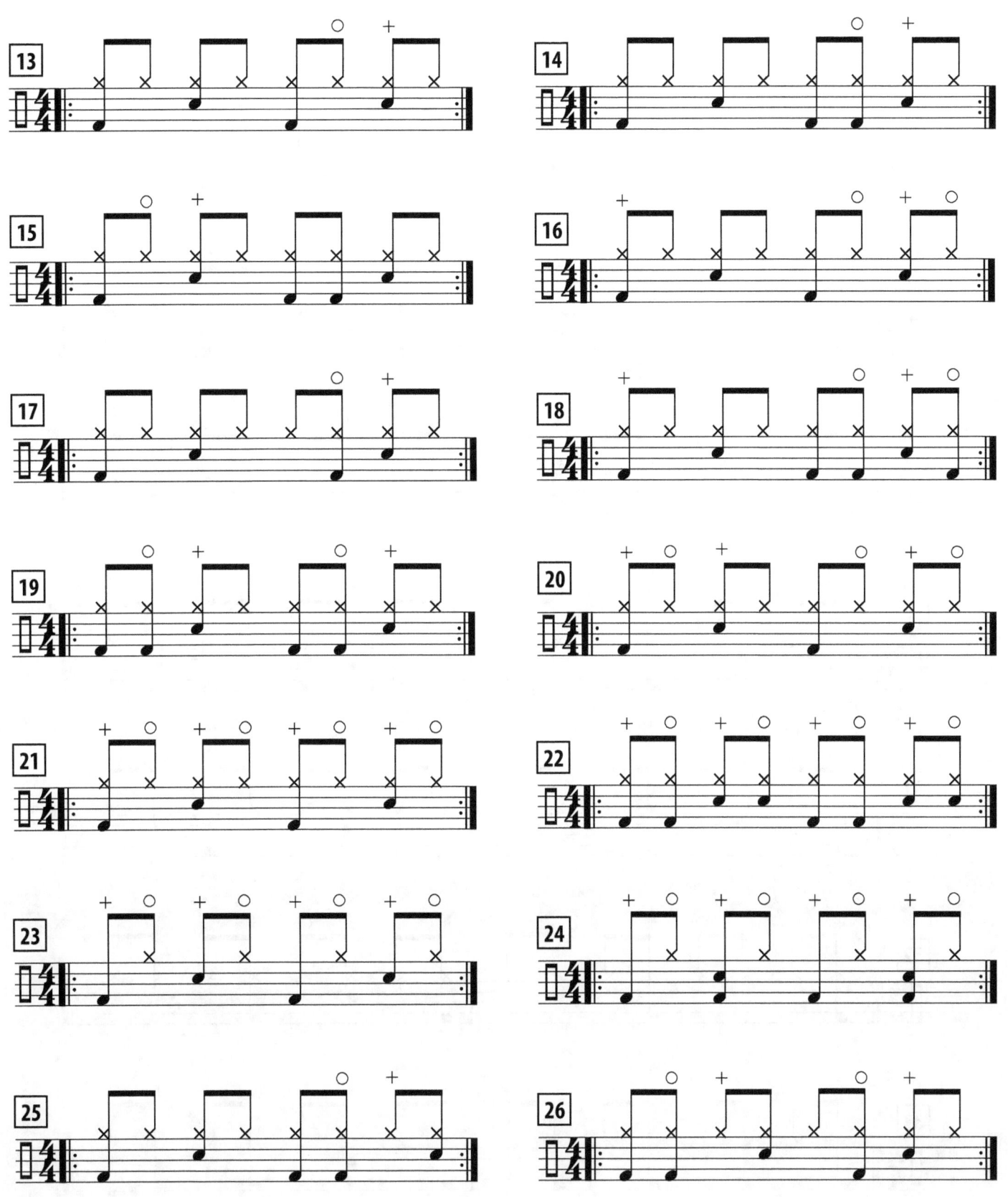

59

Lesson 11 | Opening the Hi-Hat

■ Two Measure Phrases

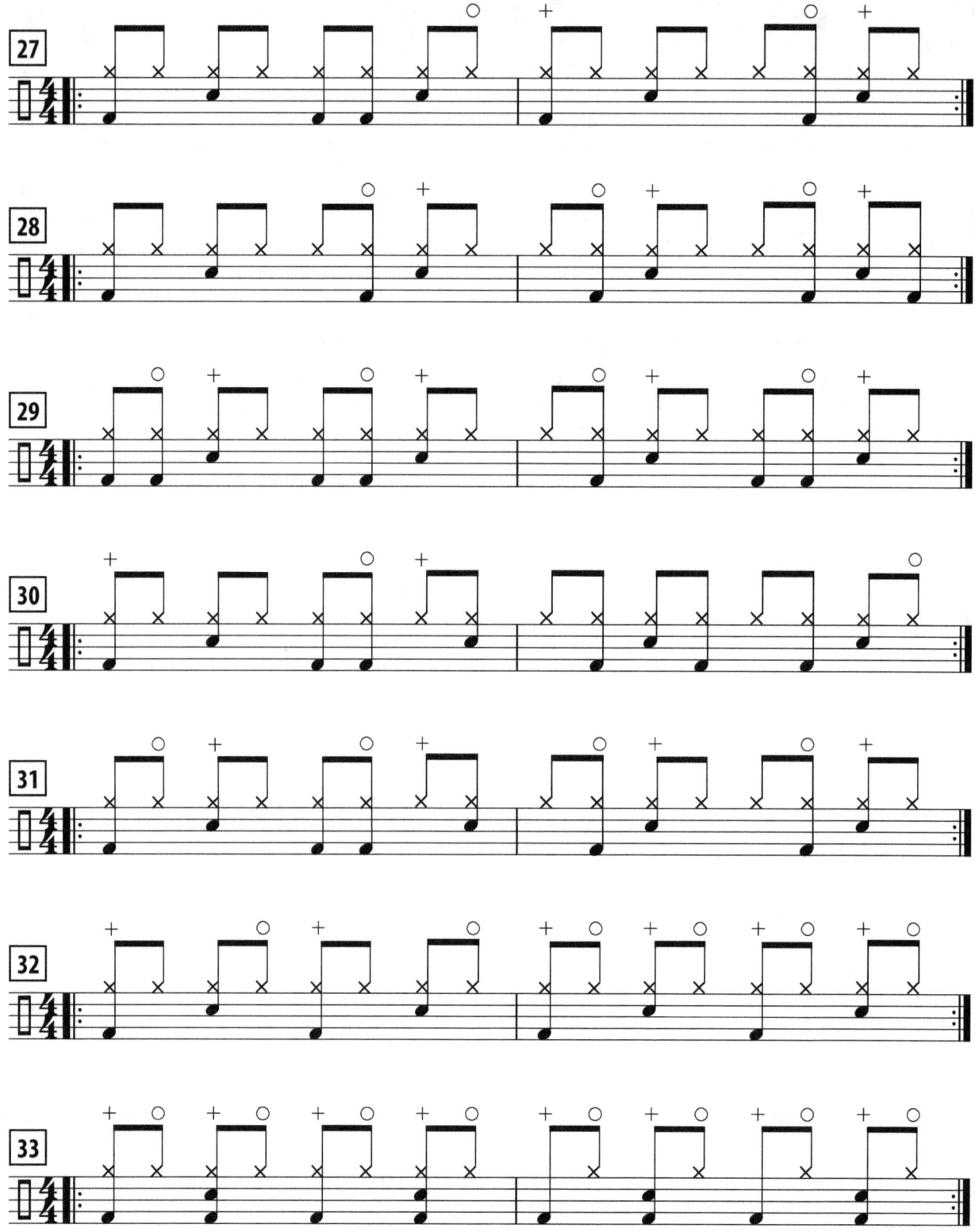

Lesson 12
Fills

A fill is a short rhythmic pattern that serves as a 'break' between grooves. This lesson will build fills using the *single line rhythm* concepts from Section 1, now assigning these rhythms to multiple drum set components. Most of the fills from this lesson can be comfortably played with a *single stroke sticking pattern* (**RLRL**) - several exercises contain printed sticking patterns to help reinforce this concept.

Practice Examples

The three examples below provide suggestions for how the following fifty fills may be effectively practiced. Notice that examples B and C feature a crash cymbal on beat 1, following the fill.

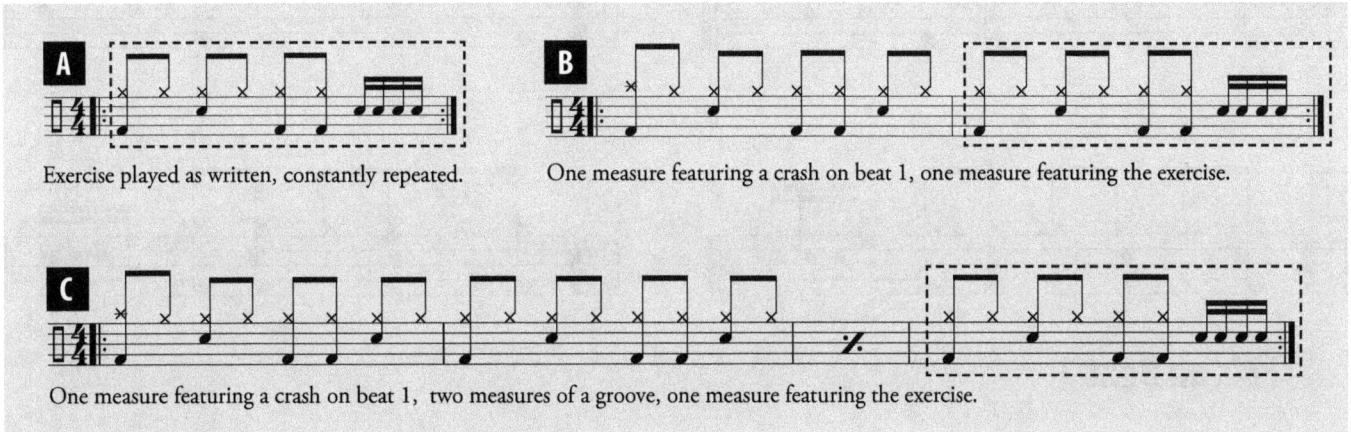

Fills on Beat 4

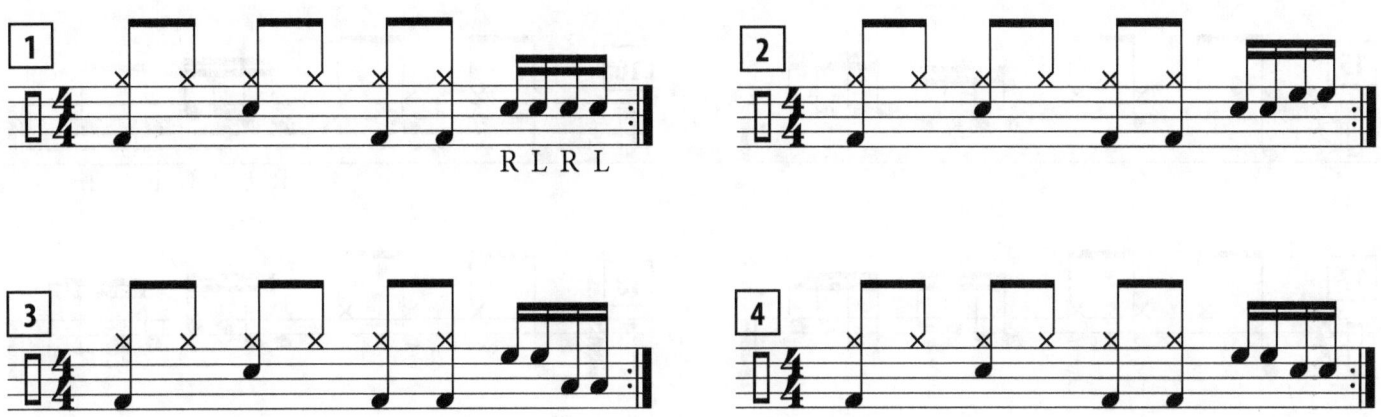

Lesson 12 | Fills

Fills on Beat 3

Lesson 12 | Fills

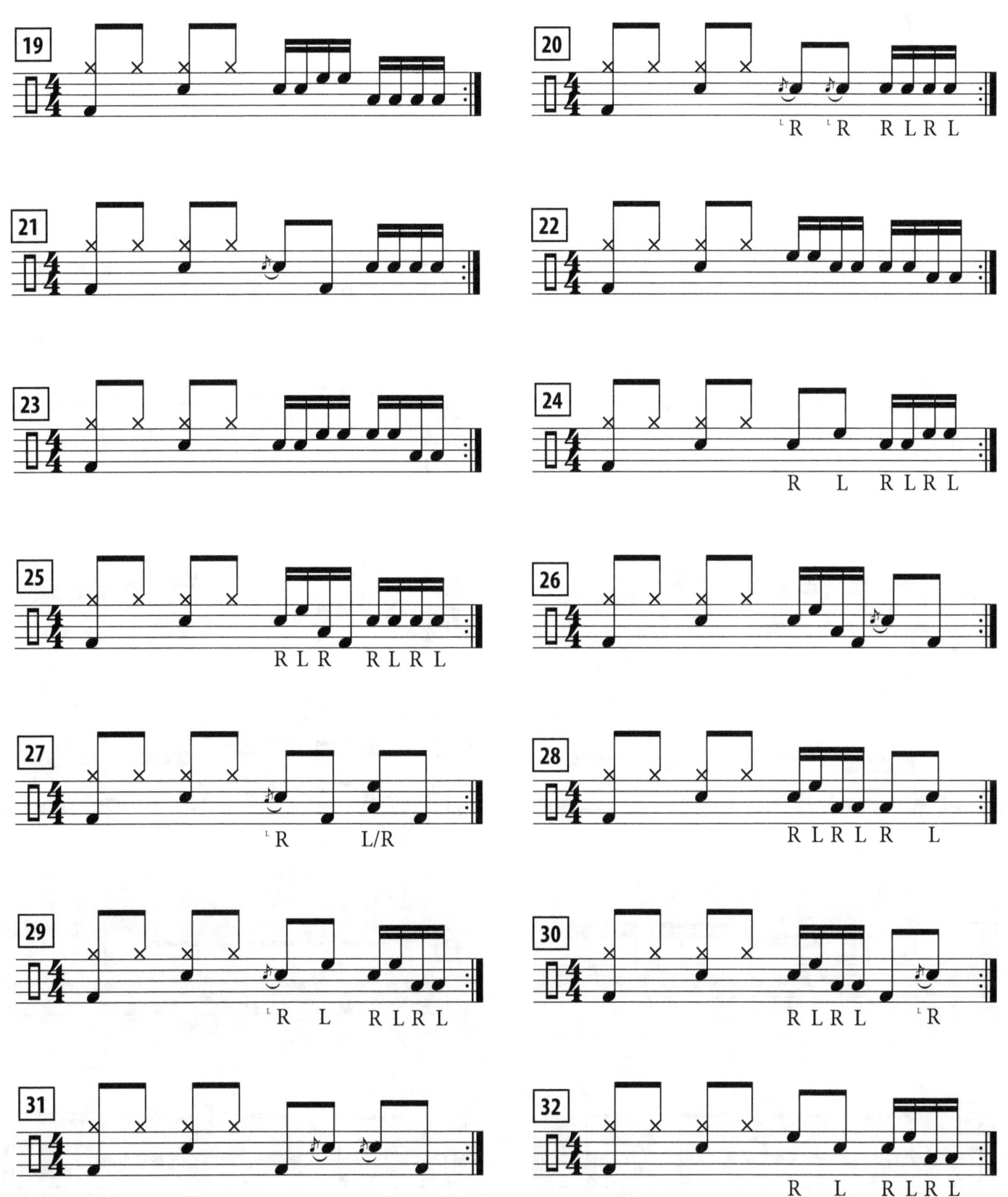

Lesson 12 | Fills

Full Measure Fills

Exercises #33 - #58 should be practiced by adding a groove *prior* to playing the full measure fill, as seen in examples B and C on page 61.

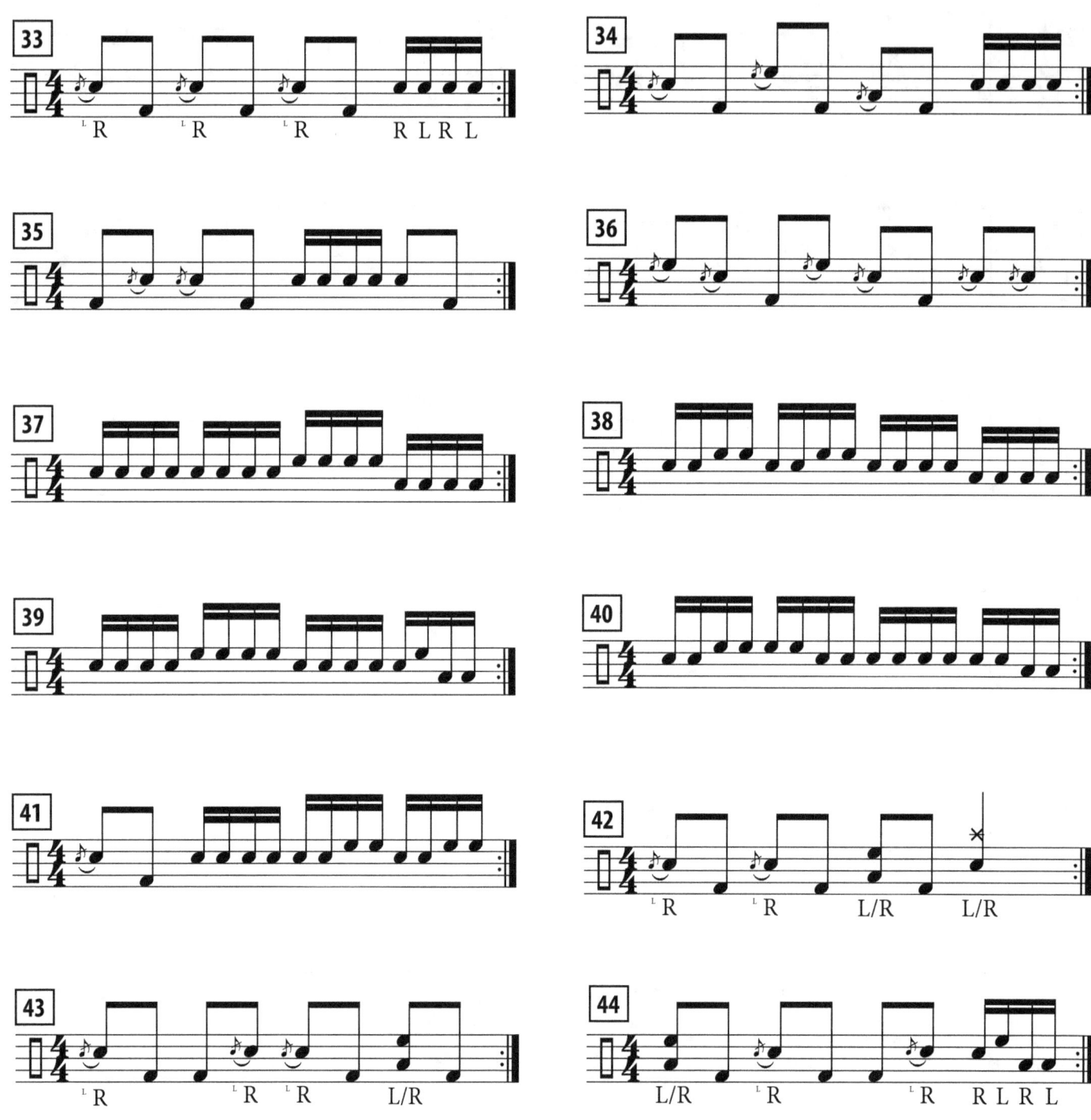

Lesson 12 | Fills

Lesson 12 | Fills

■ *Journey Through The Rhythms* with Fills

Exercises #59-#62 revist the *Journey Through The Rhythms* exercise from Lesson 8, now using a fill to transition from rhythm to rhythm. Although fill suggestions are given with each exercise, previous fills from this lesson can be used within the highlighted areas. Notice that a crash cymbal has been placed on beat 1 of each new rhythm, following the fill.

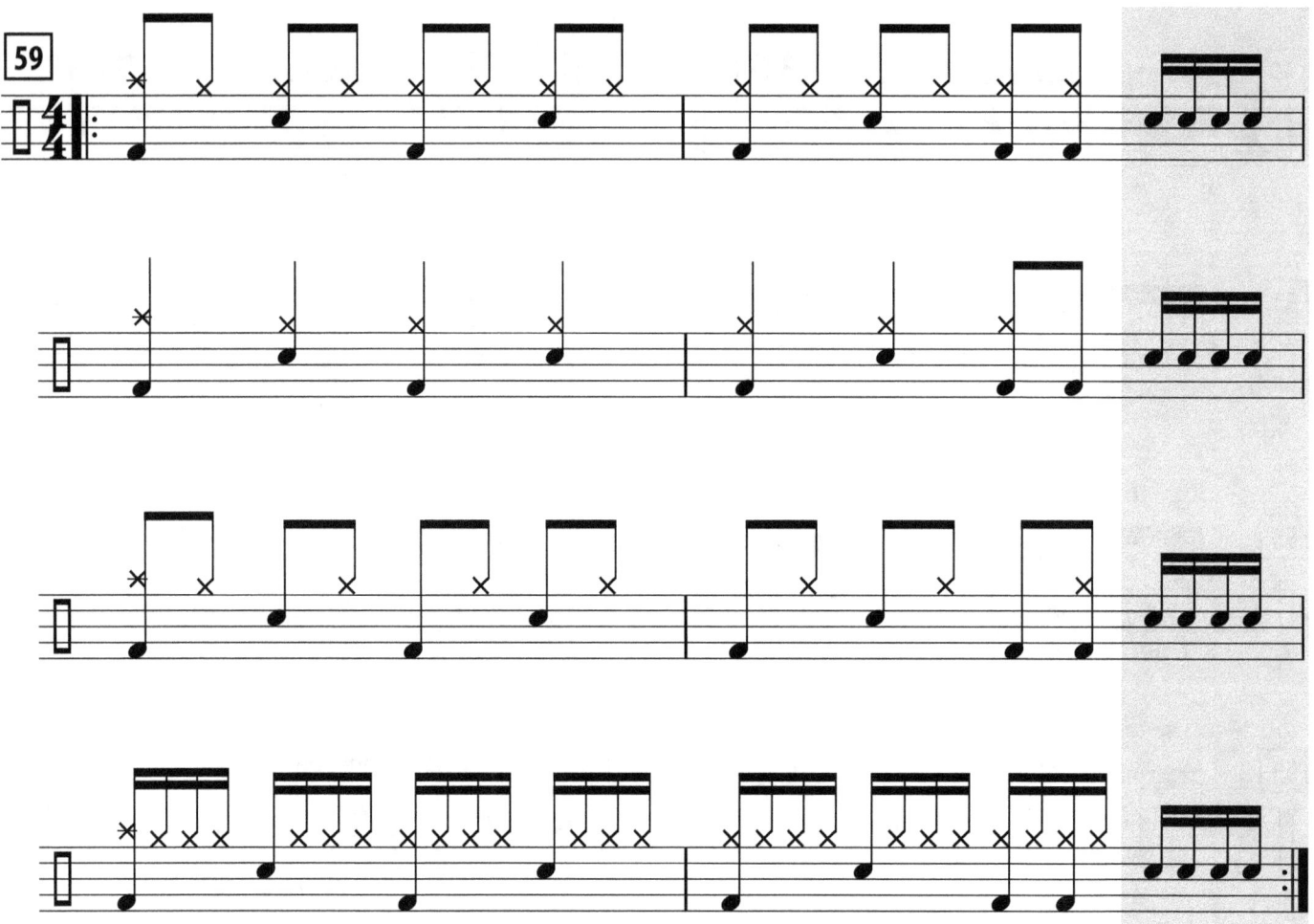

66

Lesson 12 | Fills

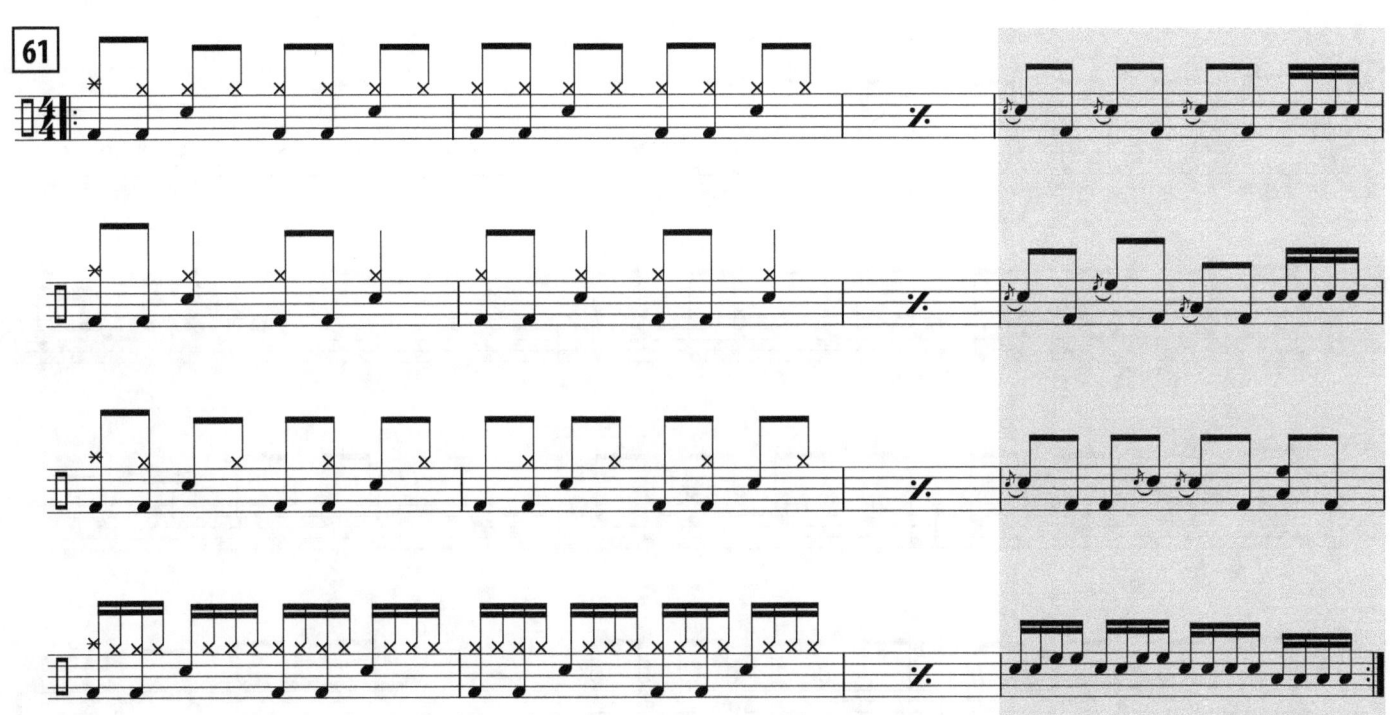

Lesson 12 | Fills

Exercise #62 features a different drum set component assigned to each rhythm.

Exercise #63 uses fills to transition between the *rhythmic feels* from Lesson 9.

SECTION 4: Drum Set Solos

Twelve short solos are provided in this section that combine all concepts discussed in this book. While every concept from each solo has been taken directly from exercises in previous lessons, several new grooves are introduced and seen in the solos for the first time. A few new ideas and notations are also featured within the solos, and have been highlighted below.

Double Repeat Signs

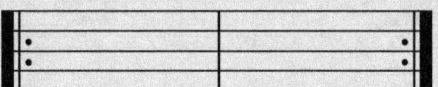

When several measures are contained within two repeat signs, the measures are to be *played twice* within the solo.

Suggested Tempo

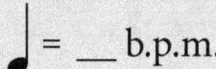 = __ b.p.m.

Each solo contains a suggestion for how many *beats per minute (b.p.m.)* a metronome should be counting. The metronome should be set to count *quarter notes*, serving as the *pulse* within each solo.

Numbered Measures

Every measure is numbered at the start of each line, allowing for the ability to quickly identify a measure or group of measures within each solo.

Alternate Notation

Some of the solos have been purposely written with a different notation style than most exercises from previous lessons, including *Hearing Voices*, which uses two different styles of notation, and *A License To Drive*, which features several of the bass drum notes written with the stems facing down.

A Simple Dish

Joy Ride

A License To Drive

The Sloth

25 Cents

A Quick Switch

Sector 7

Somewhere In Time

♩ = 110 b.p.m.

The Dryer

♩ = 120 b.p.m.

Hearing Voices

♩ = 110 b.p.m.

The Graduation

♩ = 100 b.p.m.

Space Maintainer

Foundational Drumming, Level 1 | Completion Checklist

SECTION 1

- [ ] **Lesson 1** - Quarter Notes and Eighth Notes _____ Date
- [ ] **Lesson 2** - Rests _____ Date
- [ ] **Lesson 3** - Sixteenth Notes _____ Date
- [ ] **Lesson 4** - Rudiments and Sticking Patterns _____ Date
- [ ] **Section Completed** _____ Instructor Signature _____ Date

SECTION 2

- [ ] **Lesson 5** - Eighth Notes on the Hi-Hat _____ Date
- [ ] **Lesson 6** - Quarter Notes on the Hi-Hat _____ Date
- [ ] **Lesson 7** - Off-Beat Eighth Notes on the Hi-Hat _____ Date
- [ ] **Lesson 8** - Sixteenth Notes on the Hi-Hat _____ Date
- [ ] **Lesson 9** - Rhythmic Feel Variations _____ Date
- [ ] **Section Completed** _____ Instructor Signature _____ Date

SECTION 3

- [ ] **Lesson 10** - Playing the Crash Cymbal _____ Date
- [ ] **Lesson 11** - Opening the Hi-Hat _____ Date
- [ ] **Lesson 12** - Fills _____ Date
- [ ] **Section Completed** _____ Instructor Signature _____ Date

Completion Checklist | *Foundational Drumming, Level 1*

SECTION 4

- [ ] **A Simple Dish** — Date
- [ ] **Joy Ride** — Date
- [ ] **A License To Drive** — Date
- [ ] **The Sloth** — Date
- [ ] **25 Cents** — Date
- [ ] **A Quick Switch** — Date
- [ ] **Sector 7** — Date
- [ ] **Somewhere In Time** — Date
- [ ] **The Dryer** — Date
- [ ] **The Graduation** — Date
- [ ] **Space Maintainer** — Date

Section Completed _____ _____
Instructor Signature   Date